D1532492

Praise for *The Balanced Wealth Approach*

"I started Fountain Life and wrote the book *Life Force* to bring longevity to the world. Tom Hine is furthering this important work with his terrific new book *The Balanced Wealth Approach*. Tom shows you how to mind your health as well as your wealth. Cutting edge and a must-read."
—Peter H. Diamandis, MD, XPRIZE and Singularity Founder, *New York Times* Bestselling Author

"Infused with personal insights and tried-and-true actionable steps to secure adding not only years to life but also life to your years as you build wealth, *The Balanced Wealth Approach* is sure to profoundly impact readers and their families for generations to come. Tom Hine has helped to remarkably redefine generational health and wealth with practical and powerful tools that are rarely communicated from the financial services, wealth management, and estate planning industry."
—Hector Lopez, MD, CSCS, FISSN

"Tom has raised awareness of the critical issues in health and wellness that are often ignored. He brings an innovative and actionable approach to achieving our best health in longevity. Tom brings forth critical steps and solutions to those who recognize that 'diversification in health is as important as diversification in wealth.'"
—Dr. Marien Zanyk, PhD CEO, ZANEEZ® Health & Fitness, Inventor of AnkleSTONE®, BedROK®, WillowWORX®

THE
BALANCED
WEALTH
APPROACH

THE BALANCED WEALTH APPROACH

SECRETS TO LIVING LONG AND LIVING RICH

by Thomas J. Hine
CFP®, MBA

Worth®

Securities and advisory services offered through
Commonwealth Financial Network®, Member FINRA,
SIPC, a Registered Investment Advisor.

Publisher by Worth Books, an imprint of Forefront Books.
Distributed by Simon & Schuster.

Library of Congress Control Number: 2022914875

Print ISBN: 978-1-63763-162-1
E-book ISBN: 978-1-63763-163-8

Cover Design by Faceout Studio/Tim Green
Interior Design by PerfecType, Nashville, TN

DEDICATION

For my mom for teaching us all the great
life lessons—about living a healthy life
and being proactive about health.

Most importantly, for teaching us about God
and the Unfailing prayer to St. Anthony.

For that fateful bet in 1979 when you agreed
to quit smoking cold turkey and I agreed to
start eating salads—also for that first Okinawan
martial arts class you enrolled me in that started
me on my amazing martial arts journey.

Aging is the process whereby time becomes more valuable than money.

—David A. Sinclair, AO, Ph.D.

CONTENTS

CONTENTS

www.thebalancedwealthapproach.com

FOREWORD

While many financial advisors focus primarily on the health of their clients' portfolios, there is a smaller group of advisors who are interested in their clients' overall health and well-being. Tom Hine is a member of the latter group.

Tom has been a participant in The Strategic Coach® Program, my workshop program for successful entrepreneurs, since 2004. I have been a coach to entrepreneurs, thousands of whom have been financial advisors, since 1974 and founded Strategic Coach® with my wife and partner, Babs Smith, in 1988.

Over the years, seeing the way that regenerative medicine is growing exponentially, we've expanded our focus on health and wellness, collaborating with entrepreneur and innovator Peter Diamandis to create the Abundance 360 conference, where cutting-edge technological and medical breakthroughs are shared by experts in their field, and adding a new program for our clients that's focused entirely on exploring the latest breakthroughs in health and regenerative medicine. Tom was the first client to sign up for this new program.

I had the opportunity to really get to know Tom during Peter Diamandis's recent Abundance Platinum Longevity Trips where, over five-day periods, Peter brought in thirty of the most advanced thinkers in the area of regenerative medicine. We had a chance to meet top scientists and entrepreneurs in the fields of health and longevity, and I was amazed by the depth of Tom's understanding of these topics.

I believe that financial and wealth advisors can also be key health guides. The vast majority of successful, affluent, and wealthy individuals around the world are men and women who are business owners, partners, shareholders, or top corporate managers. All of these individuals have the resources and means to also be much healthier.

Among the many advisors and specialized consultants that these successful, affluent individuals require are highly knowledgeable financial and wealth advisors. This has been increasingly the case in relation to money matters. And now it is equally the case in health and fitness matters.

I'm noticing more and more of my clients who are top advisors are combining health and wealth in their work with their clients. After all, wealth has no meaning if you don't have health. And based on my forty years' experience coaching thousands of entrepreneurial financial advisors and having personally stayed informed about the latest medical breakthroughs, I see Tom as the best cutting-edge role model for a wealth advisor who is also a guide to great health.

In *The Balanced Wealth Approach*, Tom brings together his expertise in both areas to advise readers on how to increase their health and wealth to live rich, long lives.

Dan Sullivan
Cofounder and president of Strategic Coach®

INTRODUCTION

One winter morning in 1987, my father got up and announced to my mother that something was wrong with his feet. Dad was a type 2 diabetic, so staying aware of his feet was very important—especially during a really cold winter. His feet were indeed blue, and Dad said they felt funny. Mom said, "Well, let's wait a while. It's cold out, after all." But a few hours later, Dad said his feet were still blue and still felt funny, and my father is not a person to complain about *anything*. So when he mentioned it a second time, Mom paid attention.

They went right away to his primary care physician, who didn't know what the problem was, but he knew there was a problem. He didn't want to alarm my parents, but he knew discoloration was a bad sign. In a manner he hoped was casual yet persuasive, he sent Dad to the Joslin Diabetes Center in Boston, which had a podiatrist on staff named Dr. Geoffrey Habershaw. He was *way* booked up, and his staff said Dad could see him next month. Mom implored, "*Please*, I don't care what time it is, what day it is, I don't care about anything—but can you please squeeze him in? I think it's important. The man never complains, and he's told me about his feet twice. I know something is wrong, and we need to see Dr. Habershaw."

The pleading worked. The staff gave Dad an appointment within a few minutes, and Dr. Habershaw looked at his feet. He acknowledged there was a problem and sent Dad upstairs to another doctor, a vascular surgeon. My mother, a bright and savvy woman, realized instantly that a recommendation to see a vascular surgeon suggested trouble. "We'll go right away," she vowed. My father was also bright and savvy but, being a typical man, tended to brush off risks to his health. "There's no rush, Peg," he said, but my mother insisted, and they immediately went upstairs.

Although Dad was given time with the doctor that day, the waiting room was crowded, so they had to wait some more. Then they were sent to an examining room where Dad put on a hospital gown, and they waited again. After a while, Dad said, "I can't wait any longer. I have to get back to my office."

"*You can't do that*," Mom said. She picked up his clothes, went to the door, and said, "If I see you moving, I'm going right out this door with these clothes, because you're waiting for this doctor."

Dr. Gary Gibbons, the vascular surgeon, came in and examined Dad, listening to his heart and feeling his abdomen. Within five minutes, he said, "This is very serious. You have an abdominal aortic aneurysm." In other words, the main blood vessel leading from Dad's heart had developed a weakness in its lower stretch and was extended out like a balloon. The doctor said this aneurysm was quite big and about to burst. Dr. Habershaw, the podiatrist, had known there was a problem because of the way Dad's feet looked. The "funny feeling" Dad had reported was due to the change in blood flow from the area of the aneurysm.[1] Dr. Habershaw saved my father's life.

"You are lucky," Dr. Gibbons said. "A lot of people with aneurysms don't show any symptoms until the aneurysm bursts and they collapse. You are *very* lucky."

He told Dad he had to have major surgery and instructed him not to leave Boston because the surgery wasn't going to happen for a few weeks. If the aneurysm began to tear, he'd need to go to Dr. Gibbons's hospital for the repair. If he went home to his small town, there wasn't a nearby hospital that could treat him, and he'd die. He was to stay in Boston and move as little as possible. No work. No travel, which was part of his work. No swimming, which was his normal exercise. That threw a lot of fear into Mom and Dad. But he hung on until the surgery—the surgeons had to repair *three* abdominal aortic aneurysms; they did so successfully—and he spent several weeks in the hospital. Afterward, he recuperated at home for three months.

And then he was OK.

My father survived a life-threatening medical situation because several factors fell into place:

- He recognized something was different about part of his body.
- He alerted someone else about his condition.
- He sought medical attention.
- When routine medical attention wasn't sufficient, he and his advocate (my mom) insisted on timely care from a specialist in a larger city.
- That specialist recognized his condition needed the attention of *another* specialist and sent him to a physician who could correct the problem.
- The specialist who could correct the problem gave him good advice.
- Dad followed that advice.
- A skilled physician corrected the problem.

Had Dad kept his discomfort to himself and not sought care from a specialist in Boston, he would have died from a burst aneurysm. Because he and Mom paid attention to warning signs, followed their instincts, were patient when they had to be but insistent when they needed to be, and because they had access to good healthcare, Dad had a good outcome. He enjoyed many more years with his family, including the arrival of his grandchildren.

But everything noted here had to go right for my father to survive. How many people have died because they were stubborn or self-denying or unwilling to travel, and how many patients have fallen through the cracks because doctors were overburdened, less perceptive in their work, and more prone to mistakes? My father's experience taught me, early in my financial career, that *looking out for* your health and taking whatever steps needed to *maintain* your health are paramount concerns for every adult. The insight I gained from my dad's brush with death, which happened in my twenties, has informed the rest of my career.

Tools for Taking Control of Your Health and Wellness

When I'm speaking to an audience of businesspeople—and the COVID-19 pandemic pushed this to the forefront—I tell them they need to take control of their lives in terms of health and wellness, and I can give them the tools to do it. What makes me an expert? Because for forty years I have balanced building a solid investment business and maintaining my great health along the way. In fact, a recent epigenetic test on aging conducted by Fountain Life, which I'll discuss later, calculated my physical age to be forty-four. Not bad for a guy who's sixty-one!

I tell the audience there are simple tools that will allow them to take more control over their health and wellness routines *starting today*, and they're all in this book.

One is *meditation*. I generally ask how many people in the audience have a regular meditation practice, and a small percentage raise their hands. My practice of daily meditation, which can be as little as five minutes, has been the most valuable freebie I've ever taken advantage of. My daily meditation allows me to take a break from my thinking mind, slow down my physical body, and renew the energy and clarity I need to prepare for the rest of the day.

We also discuss their *diets*, knowing that executives are often strapped for time and sometimes rely on quick meals that are less nutritious. Because food fuels your brain as well as your body, we talk about easy ways to improve their diets. One simple method is to track what you eat, then look for a diet that has been proven effective scientifically and stick to it. The scorecard in chapter 6 allows you to rate yourself in several categories, including diet and exercise, so you will be able to track yourself periodically while you monitor key financial-planning categories.

The next thing is *exercise*. I ask how many people in the room make working out a priority over their day jobs, and I find that very few do. When I create my daily schedule, I plan exercise first. A workout is whatever you want it to be. It can be stretching, yoga, walking, jogging, running, boxing, lifting weights, or using cardio equipment at the gym, as long as your goal is to exercise six or seven days a week. In my case, now it's a combination of martial arts, yoga, and boxing.

"How many of you check your health and wellness regimen as often as you check the status of your 401(k)?" is another question for my audience. Only about five hands out of five hundred go up. "Well," I tell them, "you need to check on your health as often as you check on your money." For example, many people in my audiences don't visit their primary care physicians at least once a year *with a game plan*: specific questions and concerns they have and goals for what they want to achieve based on the annual physical. When they see specialists, they aren't ready to coordinate their care among their doctors and between the doctors and themselves. Physicians are overwhelmed these days—they were overwhelmed before the COVID-19 pandemic. Patients need to be more proactive because their doctors are busy.

In short, I tell the audience they have the power to take control of their lives and not spend so much time worrying about money. The money is important, but your life comes first, and you can't enjoy what money can bring if you're ill or dead.

This book will provide the tools you need to look after your health and wellness as diligently as you keep tabs on your money, both now and for the future. If you have both, your retirement years can bring you enjoyment and fulfillment. Now, let's see how to get there.

CHAPTER 1

What Good Is a Seven-Figure Portfolio If You're Six Feet Underground?

When my dad had his surgery to correct aortic aneurysms, which I discussed in the introduction, I was a twenty-six-year-old MBA student studying for a final exam in accounting at the University of Connecticut. It was hard to concentrate. While I sat for that exam, my father would be undergoing major surgery to insert a Dacron sleeve around his aorta. Only weeks before, Dad had received a terrifying piece of news: without corrective surgery, his aorta could burst at any moment, killing him instantly.

I called my mom before the exam to assure her that the minute I finished, I'd race over to the hospital to be with her and with Dad as he came out of surgery and into recovery. At least, I hoped and prayed he would be in recovery. This surgery had a sobering mortality rate of 12 percent, even among otherwise healthy patients. If Dad's damaged aorta burst on the operating table, even in the presence of an experienced vascular surgeon, there would be nothing they could do. It would be game over.

But the surgery was a success, and my father enjoyed many additional years of life. As a side note, both my dad and Dr. Gary Gibbons really loved golf. To thank the surgeon, Dad gave him a golf club as a gift, and years later, the doctor wrote a letter to my mother—a letter she still has—saying that my dad had been one of his favorite patients because of their shared love of golfing.

Why did I begin this story in the introduction, and why am I continuing it now? Because it is a real-life example of the power of preventive medicine and of the urgency with which you must take a more active role in your own health preservation and enhancement. Many things had to go right in this situation to prevent my father's life being cut off years prematurely. First, he had to keep up with his annual physical exams. Second, his doctor had to pay close attention to my father's body during those exams—even to my father's toe—to alert him that something more serious was probably going on that required a vascular surgeon. Third, my mother had to be present in her loving, assertive way and take the bull by the horns to schedule the appointments with Dr. Gibbons. Without this trifecta of circumstances, along with others, our family almost certainly would have been robbed of many years with my father. Dad would never have met his three grandkids, gone on a Mediterranean cruise, celebrated several Father's Days with me golfing on Cape Cod, taken our seventeen-foot center console Boston Whaler out on the water, or enjoyed a number of other joyous experiences.

Not everyone is as fortunate as my father was. As a financial planner, I have been privileged to consult with thousands of clients, guiding their investment decisions that have helped them amass considerable net worth. I have done this work with satisfaction and pride for more than forty years. Too often, though, I have made a routine call to a client for a general chat or to follow up on a previous conversation, only to learn from a bereaved spouse that my client had suddenly passed away. These were not deaths through natural disaster, accident, or violence. These were all preventable deaths among good, ambitious people—usually men—whose drive to succeed in their professions and to build their financial portfolios cost them their health. They kept up with the latest news in their professional worlds and followed my advice on financial-investment strategies. Yet tragically, they had no investment strategy for their physical health or for living a more balanced life.

This lopsided prioritization on career growth and wealth creation over their health literally killed many of these clients. Some were only in their fifties, some in their sixties, and some in their early seventies. But today, the average life expectancy is seventy-seven years, according to 2020 data from the Centers for Disease Control and Prevention.[2] Most of these clients lost out on precious years—even decades—of life with their families. They had plenty of money by the end, but as we all know, you can't take it with you. Their widowed spouses had loads of money left to them . . . but no one to enjoy it with.

So what business does a financial planner like me have in writing a book about physical health? It's quite simple. Over my four-decade career, I know that my rock-solid commitment to physical health and balance has been absolutely crucial to my well-being—not just my physical well-being but also my psychological, emotional, and, yes, financial well-being.

Wealth in an investment portfolio is useless if you're not around to enjoy it. And for years (even decades) now, we have known many of the basic truths about what habits lead to better and longer life: a careful diet, regular exercise, spiritual practice, regular health monitoring through various screening tests, and emotionally fulfilling relationships, among others. And yet, while this is common knowledge, it is shocking how many people brush off these health-promoting practices and values. That is why I created the Balanced Wealth program, which I will introduce in chapter 3. Balanced Wealth offers these tools for people to become active partners in the maintenance and improvement of their own health and well-being.

I first learned the enormous benefits of exercise for my physical and psychological health at age thirteen when my mother performed a health and wellness intervention that changed my life. (It's notable that my mother is the heroine once again here; it is no secret that women are usually the ones in a marriage or a family who stay vigilant about health monitoring on behalf of everyone else—sometimes at their own expense.)

In any case, I was in eighth grade and a bit nervous socially, as so many adolescents are. One day I got into a scuffle with another kid. I didn't know how to fight, and while neither of us really got hurt, that other kid bested me. My ego got KO'd. I was really embarrassed. My mom, who grew up on the South Side of Chicago, said, "You know what, Tom? I'm going to enroll you in karate lessons." Little did she realize that my class would be taught by Walter Matson, the highest-ranking American Okinawan Uechi-ryu martial arts instructor in the country. By the time he retired, he had been one of the last guys to fight in a team tournament against Chuck Norris's team. This was in 1972 or '73, the era of Bruce Lee and the movie *Enter the Dragon*. I worked my way up to a green belt, but after two years, at age fifteen, I got bored. I stopped martial arts and took up lacrosse and other sports instead. A few years later, as a freshman at the University of Connecticut, my roommate dragged me to a Shotokan karate class, and I never looked back. I was hooked on it again, this time for life. To this day, I am still friends with that roommate. I can never thank him enough for taking me to that class.

I began my Shotokan training at the University of Connecticut under Sensei Robert Jacobs. Later, as I progressed through the ranks, I also trained simultaneously under Sensei Masataka Mori in New York City for over thirty years. Sensei Masataka Mori, who passed away in 2018, is still considered to be one of the top Shotokan Masters of all time.

My karate practice influenced my approach to wellness, diet, nutrition, exercise, study, and work. While Shotokan karate is based on Buddhism, by no means were we sitting around chanting and lighting incense. Back then, I was a normal college kid, grabbing beer and pizza with friends on Friday nights after practice. But nothing felt better than that "runner's high" we all experienced right after karate practice. I became addicted to that adrenalin rush and the release of all those feel-good endorphins coursing through my veins. The discipline I learned in karate even transferred to my academic life. When I needed to sit and focus to study, I could sit and focus for hours.

In the mid-1980s, when I entered the world of work, karate's stabilizing and health-enhancing influence grew even stronger. These were the go-go years that novelist Tom Wolfe wrote about in his novel *The Bonfire of the Vanities.* Everywhere I looked, I saw the "greed is good" mantra of the character Gordon Gekko, played by Michael Douglas in the movie *Wall Street.* The lust for the almighty dollar pushed almost everything else to the side for almost everyone else, while I kept prioritizing my personal life and health.

I was working for a major consulting firm, and the joke around the office was that the company had flexible work hours: you could work any eighty hours a week you wanted! I was able to get permission to leave the office during work hours to attend karate and then return. Over the course of a few months, I noticed three things were happening to my coworkers who didn't exercise or train regularly. The first was that tempers flared when projects got really intense. People would say or do things that could cost them their careers. Second, many marriages got trampled. People worked long hours, weren't home to tend to their spouses, and needed outlets for their stress. As a result, many became entangled in office affairs. The third thing I noticed as a clear and consistent pattern was that all this overwork was taxing people's health to the max, so much so that people began taking personal time off to deal with their stress, migraines, or whatever other health issues their excessive work habits were triggering.

Because of my commitment to working out, I never let myself get to that burned-out condition and never needed to ask for personal time off. A defining moment for me during that year was when I was talking to a friend, an accomplished consultant. He said, "Tom, think about what we're up against. We're up against the smartest people around, people who are driven and who, in many cases, are workaholics. You can't outwork them. You can't outthink them. You can't out-schmooze them, right? But we can't possibly beat them if we aren't at our desks."

Then it dawned on me that he was right: I could never advance by being smarter or working harder or schmoozing better than any of my colleagues. That's when I began to feel as though I belonged in a Dilbert cartoon, locked in my little corporate cubicle, chained to my desk in corporate hell. I began to feel not like the proverbial hamster on a wheel but more like a caged animal desperate to escape from the zoo.

I couldn't stay in the world of corporate consulting under those draconian expectations. I knew at some point I would become an entrepreneur because I refused to fit into corporate America the way it was run in my field at that time. My last review at the major firm I worked for was in 1989. At that time, I was working on a challenging project for a major bank, easily logging sixty or seventy hours a week. I had never worked on a project like this, and I was suddenly in over my head. Sitting across the desk from me was my boss, a polished, educated European named Peter who was from the Netherlands. He said, "Tom, we love working with you. You have a great attitude, and you're a hard worker. However, I can only give you an average rating on this review. The company wants you to do better, but you can't advance at this company if you keep doing martial arts."

I was still such a newbie that my jaw dropped. I was shocked that an employer would make an employee give up his ticket to physical and mental well-being. "How could my martial arts be a drawback?" I asked him. "It keeps me healthy and balanced."

Peter replied, "Off the record, Tom, I agree with you. I think what you are doing is brilliant, and I'm happy for you. In fact, at times I'm a bit jealous, because I think karate is really cool, and I wouldn't want to give it up either." He reminded me, though, that that was his private answer. "As your boss, though, I have to tell you that the partners want you here basically 24/7, burning the midnight oil until this project is done. They don't see it as appropriate for you to take time to do anything else. You just won't advance if you keep doing martial arts."

I started updating my résumé that night.

From the beginning of my working life, I clung to the tools that allowed me to live, work, and thrive. For me, martial arts training has paid incredible, unquantifiable benefits in every way, preserving my physical and psychological stamina and paving the way for my long-term success.

Of course, I cannot claim that my martial arts practice and the energy and stamina it gave me solved every problem. After I left that big firm in 1989, I became an insurance broker and worked for an agency. I sold life insurance and investments and survived for four or five years on my own before I met up with some other brokers. In 1995, I left the mother ship—the protection of the insurance agency—to start a company with these partners.

Although I was confident of my future success, the insecurity of that time brought on extreme anxiety. I was no longer tied to a consulting firm or an insurance agency. I was launching my own career, and I had episodes that felt like I was having a heart attack from the stress. I even ended up in the hospital from one of these events. I'll never forget that, after the nurse took my vitals, she said, "You're in great shape, you must work out all the time. What you had was a panic attack."

I hadn't even heard of a panic attack before; this was a totally new concept to me. The doctor asked a lot of questions, and we walked through what was going on in my life. He said, "Well, let's review what you've told me. You are launching a new venture. You're waking up at 2:00 in the morning in a cold sweat because you're so worried about it. Your heart is racing, and you think you are having a heart attack. I'm sure it feels that way, but this is definitely a panic attack." This was a huge relief on one hand and a game changer on the other. Even though I was young and in good shape, it wasn't enough.

Anyone who has had a panic attack knows they are horrible and terrifying. I sure didn't want to have another one. So moving forward, I monitored my blood pressure and other metrics carefully to prevent them as much as I could. I also cut down on caffeinated drinks such as coffee and soda. Despite working out five days a week and having strong and healthy vital signs, I had to be aware and conscientious about my health in other ways from then on.

My relationships with my clients go beyond talking about money. They are what I call "*real*-lationships" with people I care about deeply. I talk to them several times a year. I know when there are weddings in the family and when there are funerals. I know when they buy or sell houses, get divorced, have grandchildren. I hear about the stresses that business management and money can bring and about their dreams for retirement, including plans to travel or take long-delayed vacations.

These relationships often last for decades. Naturally, I care very much about the well-being of my clients and their families. It's gratifying to see a client finally achieve a stage in life when he or she can pull back from work, relax, and enjoy the fruits of their labor. So it was heartbreaking to make one of my typical check-in phone calls to a friend and client to ask about his family skiing vacation, only to find out . . . there was no vacation. His wife told me in a voice choked with emotion that he had suddenly passed away from a stroke. He was only sixty-three.

Clients who have the financial means to live in comfort or even luxury well into their nineties should not be dying in their sixties from having neglected their health.

Because of these stories, I decided several years ago that my work as a financial advisor had to expand beyond talking about numbers, interest rates, and ROI. I wanted to offer a more holistic advisory practice in which I could discuss health issues with my clients, sharing some of what I know and have experienced. However, I was not a doctor, nor was I about to go to medical school. There were strict limits as to how much I could attempt to "teach" about health and wellness. But I just *knew* there had to be a way to offer some guiding light on health.

It took a few years more for me to gather the information I needed to offer what has become my Balanced Wealth program, but in the meantime, my goal in my practice was to raise my clients' awareness about physical self-care, at least to encourage them not to wait five years for their follow-up "annual" physical exam and blood work. Too many people end up spending the last decade or two of life shuttling from doctor's appointment to doctor's appointment, dropping wads of cash on treatments that aren't covered by insurance or for home healthcare that is beyond what their policy pays for. Wouldn't it be infinitely better to spend that time and money on a luxury cruise, a vacation home, or traveling to visit kids and grandkids?

The evidence for the need for my Balanced Wealth program added up in a manner that was fast and furious. When I was doing research for my book *The Zen of Business Acquisitions,* I visited several financial advisors in Connecticut who were in their seventies and eighties who told me, "Yeah, Tom, I really should sell my practice to you. It's been my life's work, and clearly, you know how to manage it." It was a shock to me when I learned that these people, who were so sophisticated financially, had no succession plan for their businesses. Yet before they could set up such a plan (which can take a considerable amount of time), I'd learn from their spouse that the advisor had passed away. Upon hearing the sad news, I would express my sincere sorrow and then get off the phone as quickly as I could so as not to prolong the agony of the conversation with the widow.

This happened more and more frequently until I asked myself, *What is with financial advisors?* I'd call them to help arrange a continuity or succession plan so they could enjoy their life's work and spend their money with their children and grandchildren, but they were dying way too young. It almost seemed to be an epidemic.

A particularly stunning example came when I interviewed a top portfolio manager from the Midwest who handled billions of dollars in investment portfolios. Yes, that's *billions* with a *b.* He told me about a situation where the wife of one of his clients called to tell him her husband had just died from cancer. The husband had been in charge of a billion-dollar Registered Investment Advisory firm and had also died without any succession plan. There was no one in line to take over the business. The wife asked what could be done to preserve her husband's business, but the advisor told her, "I'm sorry, I can't help you because the news of your husband's death is already out there. Those clients are already looking for another advisor." That massive account and its potential revenue stream was lost to that widow and other heirs for lack of a succession plan.

The defining moment for me came when I decided to put the pedal to the metal and make this idea of holistic financial advising a reality. I had met with a new client, a man whom I had recently absorbed into my practice through one of my acquisitions. He was of Mediterranean background, a very sweet guy. He had been a blue-collar worker who invested wisely and had amassed a portfolio as heavyset as he himself had become.

I was concerned about his health—his obesity was a major risk factor—but I had just met him and thought he might consider my discussing health matters to be intrusive. I played it "safe" and kept my focus on his investments. You'll already guess the end of this story: six months later, he died of a heart attack. His wife had all that money but no one to enjoy it with. I deeply regret not having had the courage to discuss his health with him, even if he might have taken it badly. Perhaps it might have prompted him to some action before disaster struck.

So far, I have mentioned story after story of men who "died with their boots on," still in the fray professionally, but who had failed to protect the most important asset they had: their physical health. I believe the time is right for other financial advisors to expand carefully into the role of health educator with their clients. I now sometimes joke with my clients, "I'm not a doctor, but I play one on TV," and they laugh. And I am not a health professional, so the scope of my advising is strictly limited by industry regulations and my own lack of medical background. Still, as their financial advisor, I have a unique window into the lives of my clients that naturally segues into my offering resources they can elect to use, resources that can protect and enhance their physical health.

Many advisors will offer health-related suggestions in a casual, "by the way" manner: "It'd be a good idea for you to get yourself checked out since you're telling me you are feeling more tired than usual." They don't say it in a way that suggests it could be linked to a life-or-death reality, which it is. In all my years of going to professional conferences, I've never heard anyone suggest any integration of health promotion along with financial advising. Yet we have so many tools we can suggest, operated by health and wellness companies, that are available for people who are ready to proactively monitor and improve their health and self-care. These tools can help people take charge of their health as never before and prevent potentially dire outcomes.

It's understandable why financial planners would shy away from expanding their role beyond just wealth creation. First, most of us came of age thinking, *Doctors are the ones who need to talk about health. They're the experts! It's just not my job.* Second, most financial planners are already overwhelmed trying to manage their practices, especially given the legislative changes over the past twenty years and all the onerous compliance regulations they need to deal with. The last thing they want to hear from the compliance department of their firm is that a client claimed their advisor was practicing medicine without a license. Who needs that?

On top of all that, because so many advisors are overworked, they may not be in good physical shape themselves, so who are they to talk? Basically, we were not trained to think about crossing over into the health territory, even if we had the time or were ourselves models of great self-care. Nor do we need the nightmare of a liability issue. And yet financial advisors are ideally suited to offer limited health advice because we also offer life, health, and long-term care insurance. When we discuss those policies, we are obligated to ask direct health-related questions of the client for the insurance company:

- What medications do you take?
- Do you have a history of cancer, heart disease, or lung issues?
- Have you ever been treated for depression?

We're already cruising the neighborhood of health investigation; why not use these questions as the appetizer before the entrée of introducing them to state-of-the-art health monitoring programs that will give them a jumpstart on addressing health issues as early as possible?

Here's another reason why the time is ripe for anyone in the financial-advisory field to join this campaign. As everybody knows, doctors today are overworked and overwhelmed. Consolidation in the healthcare industry has forced many doctors to see more patients in less time. They are stressed by onerous regulations and paperwork that steal time from face-to-face patient contact. How many doctors today have the time to look at the color of a patient's toe during a routine physical exam? Doctors need as many allies as they can get in the ongoing struggle to persuade people to take better care of themselves.

We can be those allies.

When I floated the idea of this concept and this book to one physician, she said, "That's such a great idea, Tom. You know, I've got two patients right now who are ideal candidates for you. They are business owners, and they are killing themselves—literally killing themselves. They keep telling me, 'I have no time, I can't hire more employees, and I have to do this work myself.' I reply, 'Your blood pressure is sky-high, and the rest of your numbers are off. What is the purpose? Why are you working so hard? You are not going to be around to see this, to enjoy any of what you worked for.'

"When I say something, I'm just the nagging doctor. But they'll hear it differently coming from you. People are motivated by money. If you suggest that they won't be able to spend their two-million-dollar IRA because they're refusing to manage their diabetes, they may pay more attention."

Earlier I described that endorphin rush I get after a karate workout. Getting that fix regularly has helped me maintain a high level of self-care and a strong desire to encourage my clients to do whatever they can to boost their health, stamina, and life balance. Even when I was much younger and had professional peers who were also young, I saw that I had more energy than they did. One guy even said to me, "I sure hope you don't drink coffee because you're already almost bouncing off the walls in the office." I just laughed and assured him that when I drank coffee, it was decaf.

As I branched off into my own advisory practice, my clientele grew faster than I'd imagined it would. I firmly believe the reason I attracted more clients and became financially successful wasn't because I worked seventy-hour workweeks but because I *didn't*. I purposefully avoided becoming a slave to my work. I put my health first. I sometimes offered evening seminars in financial planning, but I never scheduled them on a night when I had martial arts practice. That time was blocked off as sacred. Working out regularly kept me energized and focused, my demeanor calm, my confidence high. This is what allowed me to climb the ranks. Commonwealth Financial Network is the largest privately held broker/dealer in the country, and there are approximately 1,600 reps at CFN. As of June 2020, I was in the top 4 percent of advisors within their organization.

As a financial advisor who is serious about the concept of Balanced Wealth, I want my clients to grow their portfolios, not their cholesterol numbers, blood-sugar levels, weight, or anxiety. The younger you start taking care of your health and resisting the pressure to get caught up in a brutal, all-consuming work life, the happier and more successful you will be in almost every area of life. I don't want you to be that man or woman who reaches a pinnacle of career success, brandishes the title of CFO or CEO or VP like a medal, has their photograph on magazine covers, and is honored at industry banquets . . . but who is on their third marriage and whose kids don't know them.

I don't want you to be that client with the seven-figure portfolio who is six feet under.

In the coming chapters, I'll share more true stories and sobering facts that will convince you that the next investment you need to make is in your health, using my Balanced Wealth program. I'll show you in this book how to begin applying it to your life right now. I'll share with you a Balanced Wealth scorecard where you can begin tracking your standing in the areas of sleep, diet, stress, and exercise as well as risk tolerance, retirement income, and investment review. Your financial advisor can be your accountability partner for how you are doing on these metrics, and the scoring will help you determine when it's time to make an appointment with a doctor, nutritionist, or financial planner. Even if you're already taking positive steps for a healthy life, I know you'll find the scorecard concept worth your time, along with the latest research in age and aging, and how all of this could mesh with your wealth-building decisions.

Wouldn't you like to take the next step to more holistic health, both physically and financially? Good—I thought so. Then let's turn to chapter 2, where I'll tell you more about the wake-up call that started my Balanced Wealth program, years before it became a reality.

CHAPTER 2

Your Health Is More Important than Your Wealth

My mom grew up on the South Side of Chicago, and my dad was from Shelton, Connecticut. He worked at Sikorsky Aircraft Corporation, down the road in Stratford, as a teenager and remembers once meeting aviation pioneer Igor Sikorsky. My folks met in Philadelphia, and I was born west of the city in Drexel Hill, Pennsylvania. Mom and Dad loved to dress up and go into the city to nightclubs where the hosts were people such as Ed McMahon and Dick Clark.

When I was a year old, my dad got a promotion, supervising sales of wire and cable in a designated territory, and we moved to Framingham, Massachusetts. It was there that my earliest memories were formed—including one of a serious attack of croup, an upper-airway infection, that put me in the hospital when I was just starting to walk. I was in an oxygen tent for most of a week, and no one could touch me, not even my parents. And babies need to be held.

It was touch-and-go for a while, but finally the doctors essentially said, *We think this kid is going to make it.* There was no lasting damage because of the croup, no permanent disability, though I was also diagnosed with asthma and continued to have respiratory symptoms at home (mainly because my parents didn't quit smoking until I had pretty much finished high school). I outgrew the respiratory problems eventually. But the trauma of that croup attack was embedded in my body.

At age one, I didn't form conscious memories of being in isolation or struggling to breathe. My mind didn't process the experience as stress, although there are other stressful events I do remember from my childhood years. The croup, though, left its imprint on me psychologically. It caused me to be wired almost from birth to think about how my body works, to be mindful of my health.

Flash-forward almost thirty years. As I mentioned in the previous chapter, in 1989 I was part of a big national consulting and accounting firm. I was an adviser in the consulting division, one of maybe fifty consultants from a major consulting firm working on a big project for a major New York–based insurance company revamping its entire accounting system. Several key managers on the project were up for partner, so they were working unbelievably long hours, working harder than they ever had in their lives because they wanted to show the C-suite guys they had what it took to become a partner.

It was an interesting bunch of people, as consultants go. I was on loan from my firm, sent to New York along with one of our partners, a seasoned, gray-haired man who looked as if he came right out of central casting. Another partner was sent from Des Moines, Iowa. And while she looked like a typical, unassuming Midwesterner, she was a chain-smoker and completely ruthless. She'd cut off your legs and walk away while you were bleeding. Then there was a very smart guy with a slight stutter from New York. He was one of the senior managers who was trying to make partner, so he really put in the hours. All these people were type A: driven, impatient, and hyperorganized. By contrast, I was relatively new at the company, probably in my second or third year, and I was excited to be part of the project . . . at first.

We worked seventy hours a week right out of the gate, and the hours got longer from there. The firm had to put us up, so a few of us rented an apartment about two blocks from where we worked. It was near the Carnegie Deli, and we used to glimpse famous people around there all the time. Those were the days when Jackie Mason had his designated seat at the deli, and we would see him now and then.

My job was integrating the banking part of this major insurance operation with the revamped accounts payable and accounts receivable. The company—this was just before the Internet became a business fixture—was changing all its checks and check-issuing processes. I was involved in interviewing all the key people who dealt with Prudential and all their payment systems as other people on the team worked on the general ledger, accounts payable, and accounts receivable components. The most daunting thing I had to do was design a new bank check, which I had never done before. That's when I knew I was out of my depth.

That's also when my boss, Peter, called me in for a review—the review that would be my last at that firm—and advised me to give up martial arts and put all my time into the job. I told him that asking me to give up what was keeping me healthy was rather ironic. I was working with a chain-smoker, an older man who probably couldn't lift a twenty-pound weight over his head, and a guy who was carrying around a potbelly in his early thirties. They were object lessons in unhealthy lifestyles.

Peter said that staying in martial arts probably wouldn't hurt my career for the next few months, and that gave me a cushion of time to find a new career where nobody could take away what I cherished the most.

I began plotting how to get back to Connecticut and find a new career that would allow me to enjoy martial arts. Having grown up as an asthmatic, I knew every breath was precious, and it was time to go. I was sur-rounded by fellow employees who were at least as smart as I was and *were* willing to work seventy hours a week. I realized something else too: even though I was the one with asthma, it was the people I'd been working with who had no idea what it was like to feel healthy.

This happened at the end of the go-go 1980s, when everyone was clawing their way to the top and busi-ness firms held to rigidly hierarchical structures. IBM was still the business model for information processing; Apple and Microsoft had become important players, but they hadn't transformed anything in the corporate world yet. None of the entities that disrupted "the way we do things" had sprung up yet: there were no iPhones—heck, there were barely mobile phones—no digital alternatives to brick-and-mortar retailers; no instantaneous ways to send money such as PayPal, Venmo, and Zelle. There were no job search sites such as Indeed or ZipRecruiter; if you needed a job, you made a million phone calls and mailed a thousand letters. There was no Instacart; if you couldn't go to the supermarket, someone had to go for you. If you wanted to see a new movie, you had to go to a theater because there were no streaming services, no Hulu, no Apple TV. If you wanted to pay your employees, you issued paper checks. Casual Friday didn't exist yet.

The only way to get ahead was to climb the ladder and make the sacrifices everyone above you had made in family and social life, self-fulfillment, and wellness.

When Peter delivered the company's ultimatum about curtailing the activity that was keeping me healthy, I asked myself, *Do I really want to be around these people seventy or eighty hours a week and live a life in which I work twelve hours, eat a late dinner, crawl into bed, and get up the next morning to do the same thing again? Am I supposed to give up the time I need to make friends, stay fit, meet the right spouse, and start a family?* The promise was that you'd have plenty of money while you were working and in retirement: high salaries and bonuses, a generous pension plan, and an overflowing 401(k). But even in my twenties, I thought, *What good is having lots of money if you work yourself to death and aren't around to enjoy it?*

I decided that if I'm going to work seventy hours a week, I'm going to do it for my own company, not for somebody else's. More important, I wanted to work with associates and partners who valued lifestyle, personal relationships, and healthy living over making wads of money. Would I really want to be partners or associates with people who placed supreme emphasis on the financial aspect and not enough on lifestyle, friendships, and healthy living? Not for all the money in the world.

I stayed in our Hartford office for six months after the project ended, and I couldn't sleep that whole time because I realized I had to make a big move. My mom and dad sent me checks to cover my rent when I resigned to go into financial planning because I had no income and no source of clients. I still thank my mom, who celebrated her ninetieth birthday in 2022, for supporting me through that time.

For the next few years, after I was licensed to sell insurance in 1990, I was living like a feral bachelor with two male roommates, the kind of setup where mac and cheese is the fancy meal of the week. We had no girlfriends, no kids, and lived a real hand-to-mouth existence. All my time went into selling insurance and practicing martial arts, and I was getting really good at the latter, entering and winning competitions. By 1994, I competed in the world tournament in Japan, which was a great experience.

It was 1995 when I had a portfolio review meeting with married clients in their late fifties whom I'd met a year or so earlier. Steve was a small, direct guy, and his wife, Cindy, was always upbeat and smiling. I was excited because their portfolio was doing well, and I was able to show them how it was diversified and growing, and they were making money. Meetings like those were why I had gotten into financial planning in the first place.

After a while, I noticed that Steve and Cindy were sitting there looking very glum, not saying a word. "Is there something wrong with the plan?" I asked.

They looked at each other, and Steve said, "No, Tom, you're doing a great job."

Then there was a long pause. Nobody was looking at anybody or saying anything. Finally, Cindy turned to Steve and said, "Steve, do you want to tell him?"

"Yeah," he said. "Tom, I've just been diagnosed with cancer. I have about six months to live."

I was floored. Steve was wiry and fit; he didn't look a day over fifty-five. "Tell me what happened," I said.

Steve's story began the previous year. He hadn't been feeling well, so he went to his primary care doctor, who checked him out and said he was fine and was just feeling the effects of stress. He went back twice when something still felt wrong, and the doctor said again not to worry; it was just stress, and he was fine. Convinced there *was* something wrong, Steve went to the Dana-Farber Cancer Institute in Boston, one of the top cancer hospitals in the United States. Sure enough, he was diagnosed with stage 4 cancer and told he had about six months to live.

I felt hopeless, just sitting there with Steve and Cindy. What was the purpose of growing their money if he was going to be gone in six months? He was going to die without spending much more time with his children and without ever seeing any grandchildren. At the same time, I realized that part of my own work was always going to be futile: no matter how hard I worked and how much money I made for clients, I wasn't God, and I couldn't overcome death.

That experience stayed with me for a long time and caused me to rethink the role I played as a financial advisor. I wanted to help my clients develop a different road map for handling their financial planning. Imagine if the news I had for Steve and Cindy were that the market was flat and they weren't increasing their retirement funds, but I had located a doctor who could extend Steve's life indefinitely. Wouldn't they be ecstatic? Money would be of much less importance. I realized the best thing a financial advisor can do for clients is to help extend their lives and give them more happy years on earth.

By the time my first child was born in 1997, I had started to expand this conversation; I would allow clients to talk about their health in ways that weren't negative or embarrassing. Because of that, it became common for me to sit down with a client and say, "OK, I've gone over your retirement savings and your mutual funds. Now, let's take a look at your height and weight and the medicines you're taking."

I started to learn basic medical terms and details about conditions that were relevant to how much people might pay for life and disability insurance, things such as elevated liver function and bundle branch block. Those items are included in the part of an insurance application called the attending physician statement (APS), which is what your doctor submits to an insurance company to verify the applicant is healthy and therefore a good risk.

At first, it embarrassed me to ask intimate questions about my clients' bodies and health. I didn't want to ask a heavy person how much they weighed or find out what medications people were on. I felt as if I was digging into their private lives, and I kept explaining to them that somebody had to ask these questions because an insurance company wouldn't write a policy unless you answered them. They understood that.

As the years passed and I got more involved with my clients, I would ask them questions about how things were going in their lives, well beyond asking about their cash flow and where they were going on vacation. I would tell them about how I practiced martial arts to stay fit and ask them what they did as a fitness regimen. I'd talk about stress at work and ask how they handled it and, if they were old enough, I'd remind them that they didn't have to work forever. This was relevant because, at that time, an increasing number of people were damaging their health with overwork.

For example, my firm did a lot of work with software engineers at a major technology company. The typical software engineer worked a gangbuster career until around age sixty-five and then retired—and often died within six to nine months post-retirement. I'd hear stories of men who dropped dead on the golf course at sixty, years younger than average life expectancy suggested they should have, leaving behind grieving, angry widows and children. *My goodness*, I'd think, *these people worked their entire lives and died without getting any pleasure out of the money they put aside.*

I was stunned, and I asked myself if this was just the software industry; it's known to produce a lot of pressure. Or was this a widespread problem in that too many people who seemed like good, hardworking Americans never got to see the fruits of their labor? It was frustrating for me to know that I couldn't change people's health and wellness habits and didn't have the portfolio to do so even if I could. I was licensed to be their financial planner, not their doctor, nutritionist, or personal trainer.

The thing about getting so involved with health and wellness is that if you think something goes even a little wrong with your body, you think it's the end of the world. For example, in 2008, around the time the Great Recession began, I bought $15,000 worth of silver coins to gain some experience in buying commodities directly because clients were asking me about it. A big trader on the West Coast shipped me the coins by armored truck in a single heavy box, and as I hoisted them off the truck, I felt a sharp pain on the left side of my chest. I thought I was having a heart attack and made a beeline for the emergency room.

What had happened—and it took two ER visits and an appointment with a cardiologist to find out—was that I'd strained a pectoral muscle, which brought on a condition called costochondritis, an inflammation of the cartilage that attaches your upper ribs to your breastbone.

The cardiologist assured me that the pain definitely didn't presage a heart attack, and it wasn't caused by any weakness in my body. That was important to me because I was so invested in being healthy and fit and in maintaining a work-life balance that allowed me to stay that way. The universe was reminding me that there was always more to learn, that I couldn't control every aspect of life, and that something could scare the heck out of you without being as awful as you thought it was. What I had feared was a brush with death was something that could be handled with Tylenol and a little physical therapy.

I realized I was different from most people to whom I gave advice. Between 2007 and 2010, millions of people lost their jobs, homes, and life savings. People were getting thrown out of their houses and committing suicide because the value of their portfolios had plummeted. I couldn't relate to a culture in which money and physical goods were such a huge part of people's identities. If I had lost my entire net worth, I knew as long as my children were healthy, my family was taken care of, and I could go to martial arts and train, I would be happy. That's who I was at that point in life. Nobody wants to lose their money, but I knew that if I could get up every day and work out, I would be OK. I would make it.

I think it's tragic that people end their lives over the fact that they've lost money or property. Except maybe

YOUR HEALTH IS MORE IMPORTANT THAN YOUR WEALTH

for the people whose homes were foreclosed, the Great Recession was a temporary situation; most of the people who held on recouped their holdings within four or five years. I realize many of those who were overwhelmed with despair already suffered from anxiety or depression, but I was stunned by how many were ready to give up the most precious thing they had: their lives.

This is when I started to formalize what had been bouncing around in my brain for years—my theory of Balanced Wealth—and I began to take a few clients through the process I was formulating. But there were problems. First, I didn't know how to integrate this concept into my regular wealth management practice. How should I allocate my time for trying to explain my Zen philosophy of life, my participation in martial arts, my practices for healthy living? I had clients who were big into bicycling; they were already living their version of Balanced Wealth. We had already agreed it was important, and we were already spending some time discussing it, so I couldn't figure out how to account for and manage the time I spent working on this side of things with a client.

The second problem, equally important, was that not everyone was going to be doing martial arts. Some clients were cyclists, some ran marathons, and some enjoyed other activities. I added hot yoga to my own practice during those years; I loved the idea that it helps release stress. Basically, I didn't really know how to formalize a program that took in a large number of pursuits. I had all these different puzzle pieces floating around and didn't know how to put them together yet. But during the next few years, I found the connecting pieces.

CHAPTER 3

How Balanced Wealth
Came to Be

My theory of Balanced Wealth was something I'd been kicking around in my mind for twenty years. It's only recently that I've been able to fit together my long experience in financial services, my decades-long passion for martial arts, my increasingly deep study of health and wellness, and my education in Buddhist spirituality into something of a unified theory. I've been implementing Balanced Wealth in various ways for years, but this book represents the first time I've pulled all the components together. That's exciting for me— creating something new out of what I've been doing for a long time.

Balanced Wealth comes out of my years of conversations with clients, hearing about their experiences, values, and problems. All the watching and listening I've done while meeting with clients amount to hundreds, if not thousands, of interviews. That's a lot of data input. Add to that my own life story—the challenges with asthma, the home I found in karate, and so on—and there's a deep pool of material from which I can draw ideas and understanding.

As a young consultant, I was a conscientious and thorough worker, but my day really began when I left the office and headed for the karate dojo, a training hall dedicated to martial arts. I would change into my *gi*, my white uniform, and come alive in the studio. The dojo was where I felt most natural, where I experienced a holistic feeling of well-being and selfhood. That's why I left the firm; why would I give up what was making me whole? Even after 1990, when I had more autonomy as a financial planner, I loved my daytime work but started to get excited toward the end of the day, when I could leave my office and train in martial arts.

There's a quotation I read somewhere that's featured in my previous book, *The Zen of Business Acquisitions,* that I probably should have saved for this one. When asked what was most surprising about humanity, the speaker said,

> Man, because he sacrifices his health in order to make money. Then he sacrifices money to recuperate his health. And then he is so anxious about the

future that he does not enjoy the present, the result being that he does not live in the present or the future. He lives as if he is never going to die, and then he dies having never really lived.

I put that quotation in *The Zen of Business Acquisitions* because when I was researching it, I came across many advisors who were dying of heart disease brought on by their workload and life habits. I would look at them and think, *My God, you literally worked yourself to an early grave, and you didn't use any of the money to spend time with your family.*

In my first book, I wrote about a wealthy client from Texas. In the mid-1990s, he was worth about $10 million. He was the biggest client I'd had to that point. I was finding all kinds of great investment opportunities for him, doing what I was trained for, but I also handled mundane stuff such as his life insurance. When we'd fill out an application, I learned a lot of surprising health information about him. He had millions of dollars, but he wasn't making health a priority for himself or his spouse, and we never talked about health and wellness. He would flit from doctor to doctor for cancer screenings and other random checkups, but he didn't have a doctor who knew him over a long period who would notice possible changes in his health.

I was stunned by the number of health issues he was experiencing. If I had been my client, I gladly would have traded several millions of dollars of net worth to turn the clock back to before those issues appeared. Today if you talk to someone worth $15 million who is battling a lot of health issues, you could say, "Pay me $5 million right now, and tomorrow you'll wake up in perfect health." Chances are they'd take out their checkbook. But if you went to that person ten years earlier, when they were building their wealth and had maybe $3 million in net worth, you could have said, "Give me one million today and you'll have perfect health the rest of your life," and they'd have turned you down.

That's why my mission has become to convince people that, just as they need to plan what to do with their money to make it last a lifetime, so do they need to plan their lifestyles so the vigor they have in their most productive years will last them a lifetime. Once you have enough money to maintain your lifestyle, I tell them, your biggest risk isn't running out of money—it is running out of physical health.

My financial planning practice has remained focused on current clients; I've seen to it that it never grew too big too fast. As a result, I work maybe fifty to fifty-five hours a week, while the heads of other firms put in seventy or more. I had to make peace a long time ago with my practice growing a bit slower because I was unwilling to work myself halfway to death. However, in return, I'm in as close to perfect health as a guy in his early sixties can be. I had to give up some income, growth, and visibility in my career, but the trade-off was well worth it.

Wellness coach Joyce Sunada is credited with originating the popular quote now passed around by life coaches and Internet memes, "If you don't take time for your wellness, you will be forced to take time for your illness."[3] In other words, work on possible health issues now, when you have the time and the flexibility, or the consequences of poor self-care will eventually catch up with you. You didn't have time to eat healthily, exercise, and get regular checkups because you were too busy working? Well, your working days are over. You have heart disease and have to quit—now. You have a bleeding ulcer that's going to kill you if you don't change a lot of your habits. You have stage 4 cancer and only a slim chance of making it to your daughter's wedding next year.

But that's a conversation someone is going to have with a doctor. We financial planners can't be so explicit; we can only send clients for insurance exams and record the results. We can't tell clients they'd be happier if they lost fifty pounds or quit smoking. We also have to be careful not to trigger a client with a reminder of something they're sensitive to. For example, if someone has lived most of their life with a persistent health issue, they've most likely already heard all the typical "have you tried *this*?" suggestions. We have to be more subtle.

The fact is, though, that subtle ways do exist. The results of life insurance exams often give clients the first clue that they have to clean up their acts. The insurance companies take every possible factor into consideration and have several categories that determine how much someone pays for life insurance. People in the *Preferred* category pay the least. In general, these people don't smoke, seldom or never drink alcohol, aren't on too many medications, aren't overweight, and have no family history of serious disease. They're less likely to die young, so the insurance company is betting it can collect many years of insurance premiums before it has to pay out. The *Standard* category includes most people. These are the folks who have standard habits and standard levels of health. Maybe they are a bit overweight but not obese; are moderate drinkers or smokers; are taking medication to control problems such as high cholesterol or blood pressure; and have family histories of heart disease, diabetes, or cancer.

Then there are the people whose health and habits are *Substandard* and therefore earn a rating in a higher-premium range. Their insurance costs are higher because they're seen as greater risks, meaning they're more likely to die while the policy is in effect. They are scored on a scale of risk called *tables*, and every table below *Standard* represents a 25 percent increase in premium costs. Even people who don't get rated can pay vastly different monthly premiums, as each level (and half-level; there are also Preferred Plus and Standard Plus designations) represents a big jump in cost. As it is, policyholders who are overweight according to body mass index pay 50

percent more in premiums than people the same age who are not overweight, and smokers pay up to *300 percent* more than nonsmokers.

While a financial planner can't harangue a client about health and wellness habits, that advisor can tell clients they're going to pay a lot more for life insurance until they haven't smoked for a year or have maintained a significant weight loss or controlled their blood pressure without medication. When you do that, you aren't judging the client; you're passing on information from the underwriter. We're developing other ways of delivering that information, though, including the scorecard that's part of this book.

I used to be fearful about discussing my involvement in martial arts, even though many people I knew in the life-coaching world encouraged me to talk about it. They thought it was so special that I had a fourth-degree black belt and had been to a world tournament that it would be an attraction for clients. It got easier to talk about specific athletic activities with clients when I took up yoga about ten years ago. Yoga is popular, and people are receptive to discussions of yoga, stretching, meditation, and mindfulness, especially when I talk about starting my yoga journey in middle age, not as a young adult. Also, reality shows such as *The Biggest Loser* have made it more acceptable to talk about weight loss.

These days, I'm comfortable talking to clients abor all my wellness practices, even recommending books

them to read. I sometimes tell them the story of my dad's aortic aneurysm as an illustration of how important it is to get an annual physical. I've found that if I leave the door open enough, they'll talk about their ailments without prompting. At that point, I feel I have the authority and wisdom as a longtime practitioner of yoga, meditation, and martial arts to go down that path without offending them because they're already talking in terms of wishing their health were better. I always approach these topics in a judicious and courteous way, but I do have those conversations.

In fact, as time goes on, I find people are more and more open to discussing their health problems. The Internet threw a lot of topics open and let people set up support groups and information-sharing fellowships. Social media made healthcare everybody's business and empowered people to speak up on illnesses such as cancer and problems such as alcoholism that used to be kept secret. Plus, some clients and potential clients have found that I've researched specific health-maintenance programs and want advice from me. One of my recent clients had a meeting with me during which we talked about health and wellness for an hour and his portfolio for only fifteen minutes.

I make it clear that I'm not a medical professional, but my access to some of the brightest doctors in the country has reinforced the importance of health and wellness in my own life and the lives of my clients. Put

that together with my documented success as a money person—my goal is to help all my clients save and protect their retirement funds—and people are more and more willing to trust me with personal details of their physical health.

Then there's the pandemic factor. COVID-19 has made *everyone* more attuned than ever to their health and wellness. They're learning about body processes they never thought about before, such as how much vitamin D they need and how to obtain it as well as how important vitamin D is to their immune system and overall health and wellness. They learn about the amino acid homocysteine and how it's a marker for heart failure, and how sleep apnea is related to the COVID-19 virus.

COVID-19 forced people to have conversations with healthcare providers about health and well-being, whether in the hospital, the doctor's office, or on the street. They saw information about the virus in a newsletter or on a website (much of it bogus, but most of it valid) and applied it to immediate health concerns. For the first time, people were made to be conscious of the benefits of washing their hands and wearing a mask. It became abundantly clear that we had to take responsibility for our own health. Most people trust their primary care physicians, so they were willing to express their concerns to their doctors. Because most people also trust their financial planners with the intimate details of their lives, they became willing to talk to me about health as well.

Potential clients are fascinated to hear that I'm involved with martial arts and yoga, but I don't want them to think I'm too far out there. I always tell clients, "I've been in martial arts my whole life, but don't worry—I don't chant or burn incense." They laugh, but I want them to know I am acutely aware that I'm handling their life savings: $2 million, $5 million, $20 million. I'm the first to recognize that Eastern philosophy and Western practicality don't always match up.

There's one Eastern concept, though, that I think is important for Westerners to understand, and that's the idea of the "monkey mind." It's a Buddhist term that refers to people who are unsettled, confused, and indecisive. Those who change their opinions all the time and jump constantly from one focus of attention to another are said to be dominated by the monkey mind. The monkey, with its excitability and shifting attention, symbolizes the human mind's waywardness. The discipline of many Eastern systems allows a person to achieve the composure the monkey lacks.

As a kid with ADHD, I was a walking example of the monkey mind. My first martial arts teacher, Walter Matson, told me when I was around fifteen years old, "You will know when you are progressing in your martial arts career when you can go through a whole class of martial arts and not think about anything but martial arts." I understood what he meant, but I couldn't imagine blocking out everything except my karate moves. Go an entire class, forty-five or sixty minutes, and not have one thought about what I might have for lunch or when my mom is going to pick me up?

I got there sooner than I expected, though. When I was eighteen or nineteen and a student at the University of Connecticut (UConn), I trained through a Shotokan class that was completely exhausting. When it was over, I realized that I had had to be totally involved, mentally and physically, to keep up with the class, and I had done it: I'd gone through a whole class with my mind totally focused on learning and not about what's for dinner, how much homework I had, or what time I was supposed meet my girlfriend. People would be much better off if they could focus that completely for an hour on their health and what they could do to improve it. I'll bet most people spend more time planning a vacation than they do on how they feel physically and why they feel that way.

If you are raised in the Western world, you're likely to be set on a path that's about money, success, building a career, and getting ahead of the next guy. But in the dojo, everyone is equal. It doesn't matter how much money you have or how well connected or well known you are. Similarly, when it comes to our health, we're all equally capable of taking care of our bodies regardless of how much money we have. Sure, the person with money has more access to gyms, fancy equipment, and personal trainers, but people without money can find ways to keep themselves fit. Yet I often meet clients who have lots of money but are less healthy than people who are not as well-to-do.

I would feel so good after a martial arts class—naturally tired, exhausted in a positive way. What else did I need in life? Enough money to put a roof over my head and eat healthy meals. When I was in college and graduate school, if I left class feeling really good and didn't have any muscle pulls or aches, I felt complete in life without worrying about what my grade would be on the next test. Then, as I got into my working career, my favorite time was spent after work, coaching my son's soccer team, helping my daughter start a mail-order business, and practicing martial arts in the dojo. The evening hours are when most people go home to mix themselves a drink or turn on the tube. For me, that time was when my day truly began.

I had a second life at the dojo and as I advanced in rank from brown belt to black belt to first degree to second degree, I took on teaching responsibilities. I would think, *This is so cool; I can do martial arts and I can teach martial arts, and the praise people give me for that doesn't have anything to do with how much money I make, how well connected I am, the kind of car I drive, or what my family name is. None of that matters! The only things that matter are whether I'm a good practitioner, a good teacher, and a good human being.*

That last thing is just as important as being wise and healthy. Those of us who practice Shotokan karate, which is the most familiar kind, follow the principles of Gichin Funakoshi, who helped popularize karate in the first half of the twentieth century. Funakoshi's twenty guiding principles of karate include mindfulness, diligence, resourcefulness, justice, perseverance, and respect for others.[4] Shotokan counsels nonviolent behavior, which can be a shock to people who think martial arts is all about breaking things and attacking enemies.

It also places pursuing perfection of character well ahead of perfecting one's technique. The Twenty Principles say nothing about how good your technique has to be. They don't try to imbue you with the aspiration to win a world tournament. They do intend to make you want to be the best possible human being you can become: a good neighbor, a faithful spouse, a diligent employee or beneficent boss, and a supportive parent.

Funakoshi's principles, invoked daily at the dojo, helped me realize working the numbers effectively wasn't enough for me to become a successful financial planner. I also had to be honest with my clients and faithful to the highest ethics of my profession. This psychological and emotional health combined with physical health is a crucial element of Balanced Wealth.

The strongest support for healthy living, though, has to be exercise: You must move your body to keep it healthy. Scientific studies have proven for years that people who exercise more live longer. Sure, you'll see stories about runners who drop dead in their forties and boxers who are killed by an unspectacular punch, but these situations are noteworthy because they're *outliers.* An athlete's cause of death generally turns out to be an undetected medical problem such as a congenital heart defect, not the exercise regimen itself. For the most part, moving your body not only releases feel-good hormones such as endorphins but also strengthens immune responses and helps fight off inflammation and infection.

It's my position that an exercise routine should be formalized, involving one or two activities that will help people achieve and then help them maintain a maximum level of health. It has to be something the individual enjoys doing because if they don't like doing it, eventually they'll stop. Some people enjoy going to the gym to work out; they like being with other people and find the sight of people taking care of themselves and trying new moves or equipment inspiring. Others dislike the smell and feel of the gym and would rather exercise alone, so that person needs a cardio machine and a set of weights at home. Part of the formality comes from the structure of the exercise: everything is meant to be done a certain way for a certain number of reps or a certain time. There's a correct method in almost any practice, whether it's executing martial arts moves, lifting weights, performing yoga poses, running, doing Pilates, or boxing. It should be something done at a consistent time of day, several times a week. And it should include metrics that allow people to track their progress, such as measuring blood pressure, resting heart rate, and so forth.

Then there's just plain walking, which doesn't have all the structure but gets the body moving. Many of my clients, especially the older, wealthier ones, really cringe at the idea of going someplace they don't really want to be where someone barks instructions at them. Twenty or thirty minutes per day of brisk walking works for a lot of folks, even if they don't break a sweat, and you can measure walks in terms of distance. For example, a walk twice around my neighborhood is one mile, and walking that distance within twenty minutes or less isn't a bad workout. In fact, it's what I do if I've pulled a muscle or am just too tired for a session at the gym or dojo. Sometimes, something that isn't too taxing, such as walking or *tai chi*, is the best option; after all, one of the things that guarantees failure is to put someone in an environment where the battle is going to be all uphill, and the chance of success seems unreachably remote. Any movement is better than the alternative, which is being a couch potato.

Basically, I try to help my clients balance their health and their wealth through exercise regimens they enjoy that are age- and health-appropriate, that work their bodies without injuring them, and that they can stick with over the long haul. All sorts of activities complement and support the components of the medical approach that is part of the Balanced Wealth program, and we'll discuss that in the next chapter.

CHAPTER 4

More than Money: Redefining Generational Health and Wealth

When I was growing up and well into adulthood, success was measured by how much money you made. If someone was a doctor or lawyer with a big practice, a big house, and a big car, that person was successful. The real estate agent who sold lots of houses, the store proprietor who had lots of customers, and the factory owner who employed lots of people— they were successful.

You never heard anyone say, "You know, there's this family down the street, I think he teaches at the high school. They are super healthy. They eat dinner together every night, and I always see them biking on the weekends. I went over there once to borrow a lawn mower, and he's got this whole home gym in the garage. He says his wife and kids use it too. That's what I call a successful guy."

Most people would have said, "OK, he has a gym in his garage, but he has a twelve-year-old station wagon in his driveway." But I know now what few people knew then: people who take care of themselves and who do their best to pass on good health habits to their children *are* successful. What greater gift could you give your family than the wisdom to head off health problems before they become serious? What would they treasure more than long life and health, theirs and yours, and the memories that come with those additional years?

That's why those years were so critical for me. After three years of working crazy hours I realized, *My gosh, if this is what success is, I don't want any part of it—not if I have to trade my health and vigor for it.*

We need to redefine what success is today so people don't focus only on the money aspect. The cracks are already beginning to show publicly, as in the sports world, where athletes such as Naomi Osaka and Simone Biles are saying, "I need a break. The pressure of competition and the hours of training are too much." People are starting to recognize that it's important for each of us to look after our own health and wellness, especially since no one else is going to do it for us. (I find this YouTube video of motivational speaker Mel Robbins is very helpful with her "It's up to you" philosophy (to see this video please go to www.thebalancedwealthapproach.com).

We have to find ways to make passing down *wealth* from generation to generation more than bequeathing money. A retirement or estate plan is a fine way to hand down money to the next generation, especially if it includes life insurance; if it's properly structured, life insurance is passed on tax-free. But that money doesn't come with any wisdom. Someone you're related to gets a big tax-free check and is happy to have the cash, but money is all you've transmitted.

What I'm talking about here is more like an *ethical will*, a nonlegal document in which you state your values and clarify the legacy you wish to leave your family in terms of how to live honorably and enjoy life to the fullest (to see a reference to an ethical will visit www .thebalancedwealthapproach.com). It can include family history, stories, and ideas for how the writer wants to be remembered; its tone is usually spiritual. Rooted in Jewish tradition, the ethical will is now being used by people of every ethnicity and faith community, and you can find many companies providing templates for ethical wills on the Internet. I recommend everyone generate a document that's a sort of ethical will for health, but don't save it for after you're dead. Disseminate it during your lifetime as you would an advance healthcare directive (living will).

In that kind of document, you can advocate ideas and actions that you feel are crucial to your loved ones' future health, such as these:

- Ask your children and grandchildren to commit to regular visits to doctors and dentists for themselves and their kids so they can be screened for health issues and possible medical challenges.
- Urge them to sign up for a genetic testing program such as 23andMe.com or Ancestry.com, which can provide insights into possible genetic issues, and use the information provided.
- Remind them to learn their family histories of illness and longevity, going back at least to grandparents and out to their parents' siblings (i.e., aunts and uncles).

For example, in my family, my father developed type 2 diabetes as an adult, and I had an uncle with diabetes as well. That made it doubly important for me to stay fit and not let myself go during middle age because I wanted to avoid the onset of an illness that was fed by being overweight and inactive.

Considering all the progress we have made as one of the wealthiest nations on earth, it seems a shame that we can't find a way to identify and begin to help people overcome their physical and psychological issues much earlier in life. Young women such as tennis star Naomi

Osaka and gymnast Simone Biles may not have needed to interrupt their careers as early as they did if their push to stardom had been tempered with understanding and a sense that, even as children, they had some control over their schedules.[5] What if professional athletes (and CEOs, surgeons, and so forth) had coaches who not only encouraged them to excel but also taught them how to pace themselves, care for themselves, and know when to take a break? They might not need to suspend or end their careers early; they might reach the height of their careers thinking what a wonderful ride they'd been on, ready to pay forward their success instead of burning out or losing control.

Then we have the reality that most people are *not* professional athletes, movie stars, surgeons, or CEOs. Of course, people will pay attention to problems that famous people have, especially if they admit it and recommend a solution: "I have this problem, and this particular program helped me recover." To whom are most people going to listen: the folks they play tennis with on Saturdays or Rafael Nadal? Who's the more believable proponent for a longevity regimen, Warren Buffett or the curmudgeonly old guy next door?

That presents us with a two-pronged problem. First, we have to convince people they don't have to be celebrities to benefit from a certain program, and second, we have to show that the average Joe or Jane can step forward as an example of a program's success. This is more than possible; weight-loss regimens have been doing it for years in their TV commercials.

I will say this, however: when celebrities put their problems, vulnerability, and need for help on display, they do a real service for the rest of us because it raises awareness of those problems as nothing else can. A society in which athletes publicly cry out for assistance and make us aware of our issues is a society in which regular people can do the same thing.

My goal, then, is to present you, the noncelebrity reader, with a framework for living that can serve you as well as it could serve the overwhelmed athlete, performer, or business mogul. Everyone deserves to get to the height of their career without having it all disappear because of poor physical and/or psychological health. It's as much about awareness as it is about action. I want to give you tools that will make you aware of what you're doing to your body and your soul as you work hard and sock away cash in your retirement fund, because if you aren't aware of what you're doing to yourself, you aren't going to have the active retirement you're working toward. You may develop conditions that keep you trapped at home or tethered to machines. Worse, one of those conditions might end your life before you reach retirement age. That's why tools such as the Balanced Wealth scorecard and precision medicine are so important.

In recent years, programs have come along that are meant to give you a sense of where you are healthwise that's almost on the molecular level. These business ventures allow people to track their health as they do their wealth, and probably more completely and in more detail. They represent the meeting point of medical technology, artificial intelligence, and entrepreneurship at the most sophisticated level possible—and in the coming years, that level will be higher.

One such program is California-based Health Nucleus, whose motto is "Don't die of something stupid" (that is, preventable). It was founded in 2014 by its parent company, Human Longevity, Inc., with the goal of helping people live to a healthy one hundred years old. After you sign up, the company will put you through a battery of tests to take a deep dive into your health: a brain scan, a full-body MRI, a heart ultrasound, a CT scan, and a lot of other tests; the entire battery takes about five hours. They sequence your entire genome. With the scans, they're able to see if there's a tumor forming, if there's plaque forming in your arteries, anything that may turn into something that's going to kill you. They analyze more than one hundred and fifty gigabytes of your physical data, then follow up with a doctor who can put you on the path to a healthier lifestyle. Health Nucleus also has ties to some of the best specialists in the world, including more than a thousand medical professionals at Massachusetts General Hospital.

The president of Health Nucleus, Dr. David Karow, MD, Ph.D., notes that although the healthcare system in the United States today consumes $3.7 trillion annually—17 percent of the country's gross domestic product—life expectancy has gone down recently after decades of increases.[6] Part of that loss came in the wake of the COVID-19 pandemic, but much has occurred because the health industry's focus is predominantly on curing people of illness rather than identifying and mitigating risks for preventable diseases.

For example, Dr. Karow says, doctors today might find bladder cancer but not until blood is detected in the urine, when the cancer is often too advanced to treat.[7] Health Nucleus specializes in pre-symptomatic diagnosis and is even more invested in taking action to stop common diseases such as diabetes, stroke, and cancer from striking in the first place. Its vision is to move America's healthcare system from "sick care" to well care.

"We want to be your partner in longevity and performance," Dr. Karow says. "Our vision is to change the healthcare system from sick care to well care, one patient at a time. Our goal is to get you to one hundred healthily. If we find a tumor, it's at an early stage and can sometimes be treated on an outpatient basis."[8]

This type of advanced, specialized healthcare can cost thousands or potentially tens of thousands of dollars. Prices and models of service are constantly evolving so check out the Health Nucleus website at www.humanlongevity.com.

But the advanced testing makes a couple of things possible. First, the individual who has this kind of work-up gets the broadest and deepest awareness of their health status. They find out exactly what they need to work on if something is pointing toward cancer, heart trouble, or something else life-threatening down the road.

Second, because several companies are competing to provide this kind of highly effective practice, they're creating several tests for an increasing number of people. In the process, they're competing to make these tests shorter, easier, better, and cheaper, which means the ultrahigh, seven-star service you get from Health Nucleus will be what everybody gets at their doctor's office ten years from now, when they've driven down the cost. It's analogous to cell phones: thirty years ago, only the super-rich had mobile phones and now they're ubiquitous. It's going to be the same with healthcare.

If you have the money, this kind of medical attention might be the best gift you can give yourself or someone else. Think about it: if the IRS limit for tax-free gifting (of cash) is $16,000 (in 2022), that's enough to pay someone's fee for a complete exam at one of these programs. Wouldn't the gift of a onetime membership be a real act of love? For less than the cost of a kitchen remodel or a used car, you can help yourself or someone else live longer and better.

Businesses such as Health Nucleus are integrating the available science with the funding needed to make real results out of theoretical models. They use the expertise of people such as Peter Diamandis, an investor in Health Nucleus and similar ventures, Fountain Life, and Lifeforce who trained as a physician but who has spent most of his career as a venture capitalist in the biotech community. Innovators such as Peter realize the rate of discovery and change is so fast that he's one of the few who can stay on top of it. They scour the planet for tests and diagnostics that haven't yet made their way into mainstream American medicine. And they all know one another, so they act as the glue holding together a constellation of entities that are overhauling medical practice.

They also create coaching programs so people who aren't on the cutting edge of medicine can learn about their operations. Again, these programs are expensive to attend, but people who can afford them get to learn about techniques and diagnostics that even five years ago were shared by a tiny inner circle. As this advanced information reaches a much larger stage and more people, folks like me can integrate it into the process I call Balanced Wealth. I'm introducing it to more and more of my estate-planning clients, and they are fascinated by it.

Another goal these new medical practices have developed is the concept of "longevity escape velocity": the idea that for every year you live, you'll be able to extend your life by another year. Right now, there are scientists who say we're already able to add one year for every four because of new research and diagnostics. In ten years, they're saying, the ratio will be one to one. That would add up to many, many more years of healthy life—imagine zooming past the century mark and continuing for decades longer—for people who buy into the latest advances.

I heard Peter Diamandis speak at the 2021 Longevity Platinum Conference, and he translated this idea as, "For the next ten years, don't do anything stupid that will kill you, because in ten years, you can achieve escape velocity."[9]

The idea that aging, with its accompanying conditions, is preventable, not inevitable, isn't new. In May 2010, a group of geneticists in the Royal Society of London for Improving Natural Knowledge, Britain's national academy of sciences, began to recast the way people thought about health and disease. Dr. David A. Sinclair, author of the anti-aging manifesto *Lifespan: Why We Age—and Why We Don't Have To*, cites one of the scientists, biogerontologist David Gems, who wrote a summary of the Royal Society meeting:

> Advances in our understanding of organismal senescence [i.e., aging] are all leading to a momentous single conclusion: that aging is not an inevitable part of life, but rather a disease process with a broad spectrum of pathological consequences. In this way of thinking, cancer, heart disease, Alzheimer's, and other conditions we commonly associate

with getting old are not necessarily diseases themselves, but symptoms of something greater. Put
more simply, and perhaps even more seditiously,
aging itself is a disease and the single most powerful risk factor common to all of these age-related
chronic diseases.[10]

In other words, for more than a decade now, *aging* has
become the problem scientists want to solve, not disorders, one by one, of the human body's organs.

David Gems echoes physicist and Nobel Prize lau-
reate Richard Feynman, who said, "There is nothing
in biology yet found that indicates the inevitability of
death. This suggests to me that it is not at all inevitable,
and it is only a matter of time before biologists discover
what it is that is causing us the trouble."

Sinclair also writes about a statistic called the
Disability-Adjusted Life Year, or DALY for short. This is
a measurement across a society of the disease or disability burden for a population. DALY combines the number
of years lost to early death *and* to ill health and disability. In other words, it adds two statistics that used to be
separate: years lost due to dying early and years lost due
to disease or disability. One DALY is equal to one year
of healthy life lost.[11]

Disabilities and diseases are given weighted values
when calculating their effect on a population, and part of
the calculation for years lost due to death is the standard

life expectancy at the time of death. The lower the rate of DALYs in a given country or other population, the better off that population is healthwise because lower rates of disease and disability burden suggest that there's been improvement in reducing risk factors for disability and in preventing, treating, and curing illnesses.

DALY is not an absolute metric: there are too many differences in the ways different populations regard and measure poor health. The average death rate in a specific nation varies over time, and life expectancy can be depressed by certain factors such as an active war, widespread drug abuse, or the COVID-19 pandemic. Researchers differ on whether the DALY rate in the United States is rising or falling, but it isn't good. For example, a study of twelve highly advanced nations in 2019 found that the US led the pack by a significant margin, with more than 26,000 DALYs per 100,000 population—more than 5,000 DALYs ahead of the number two nation and 7,000 ahead of the average.[12] Obviously, we want the DALY number to come down.

Now an internationally recognized metric telling us how much productive life we are losing through early death and poor self-care, DALY gives us another talking point for Balanced Wealth: we can show people how many years of life and wellness they're giving up with their current lifestyles and how they can turn that around.

It's amazing how many people are conscientious about their finances. They know exactly how much money they make and how much they have, and/or they have a financial advisor who keeps them up to date diligently. They keep careful track of where they spend and donate money. They know what their limits are—how expensive a car they can buy, how posh a vacation they can take, and so on.

At the same time, most people don't focus on their health. They die or get sick before they can enjoy their money and experience the benefits of all their hard work. They die before their family members can enjoy them and have them present at events such as the birth of a grandchild or a family cruise or a wedding. But now there are doctors who have teamed up with entrepreneurs who are saying it doesn't have to be this way. Good health as an older adult shouldn't just be trying to avoid a heart attack or a stroke; it's about staying healthy enough to enjoy yourself and the people you love well into old age. And you can do that if you take advantage of the highest levels of medical information available. You can do it if you pay as much attention to your health as you do to your wealth.

Physical wellness is something you need to commit to as strongly as you committed to finishing your professional degree, providing for your family, and making sure your parents are comfortable in their old age. There is no better gift you can give to yourself or to someone you love.

In financial planning, we often do what we call *generational planning.* That refers to taking the money that Mom and Dad worked hard for and helping it get to the next generation in a legal, ethical, and financially prudent way. For example, say your parents built up a successful business, and you expanded it; now you want your kids to get the benefit of their hard work and yours, so you work with an advisor who will grow your money before you hand it over to the next generation.

Imagine doing that with medical knowledge: getting your own genome sequenced so you know some of the health events you might face and then passing that knowledge to your kids. If you make it possible for them to take advantage of similar knowledge, what a gift that will be! You'll be saying, "Hey, kid, I'm not just going to leave money for you. I'm going to leave you a road map of how to live a longer and healthier life." Financial advisors can be part of that effort, too, if they learn about these sources of cutting-edge medical insight.

With Balanced Wealth, I want to focus on handing down the keys to the kingdom, the blueprints, the DNA, the answer to increasing the family's longevity. Imagine seeing your grandchildren become grandparents! Imagine eliminating a genetic disease from your family's future generations! This could be possible with planning that focuses on health as well as wealth.

Of course, in order to make sense of the information you receive when you commit to looking after your health and lengthening your healthy years, you need a template on which you can plot the numbers. Later we will introduce the scorecard on which you and your advisors—medical and financial—can measure your progress.

CHAPTER 5

It's All a Matter of Balance

During my research for this book, I encountered one phenomenon again and again: almost every health issue has a parallel in the field of wealth management.[13] It was uncanny!

For example, we talk about maintaining a balanced portfolio, with, say, 60 percent stocks and 40 percent bonds. That's the typical balance for someone in middle age. There are many parallels between keeping your financial portfolio in balance and your health habits in balance. Think of the stocks as your heart and your bonds as your lungs. Just because one is doing well doesn't mean you can ignore the other. Your heart may be in fabulous shape, but you can't use that as the only measure of whether you're in good shape overall.

I had a client who was overweight and smoked a pack of cigarettes a day, but he insisted he was in good shape healthwise because his heart health was good. His heart at age fifty-five was doing so well that it mystified his doctor. "I don't know why," the doctor said, shaking his head, "but you have the heart of an eighteen-year-old." Although the guy played tennis regularly and didn't have trouble with breathing, the doctor warned him that his good heart health wouldn't last if he didn't lose weight and quit smoking. But he wouldn't listen. A few months later, he came down with a cold, nothing severe, but he couldn't stop coughing after the other symptoms subsided. That lingering, hacking cough made him pay attention to his lungs. He quit smoking and began to lose weight. Today he's eighty with a clean bill of health for a man his age.

You need a balance between diet and exercise, too, if you're following a regimen of weight loss or overall well-being. Both eating the right foods and moving your body purposefully are necessary for optimum health. Some people think there's no reason to eat mindfully or exercise if you're thin. You hear about people who eat anything they want and never move, and they stay rail-thin; what you don't hear is that they have no stamina and are laid out by a bad cold or a simple ankle twist. Their muscles are underdeveloped, and they don't con-sume the nutrients that can help them ward off illness. And there are folks who work out all the time, but their diets are terrible. They aren't doing themselves any favors either.

Another parallel between health management and wealth management is the importance of metrics—hard information that can be documented, evaluated, and placed in context. As a financial planner, I look at a client's income, tax rate, and instruments that address the future: Have they executed a will? Does each spouse carry life insurance? I'll ask about financial history such as past investments, home ownership, and level of student and consumer debt. These and other factors are the key indicators I'll use to assess a client's financial health and determine the best path for that person going forward.

With those data points, I can be a more effective financial planner. I can point out someone's predilection for get-rich-quick schemes that never quite pan out; I can put someone on a financial diet who wants to live like an NBA star but has an assistant coach's income. On the other hand, I can coax a prudent but overly conservative investor into branching out a little, adding a few jalapeños to the stew, so to speak, because I know their portfolio can withstand a tremor or two in the market. What I can't do is work magic such as create an overnight fortune for someone who doesn't have much in financial holdings, or send someone back in time, say, to buy Zoom at $36 per share in April 2019 (*before* COVID-19).

It's the same with health. Any advice a doctor gives you is going to be based on a comprehensive medical history and current metrics: blood pressure, heart rate, measures of liver and kidney function, plus levels of cholesterol, enzymes, and hormones. The doctor will find out your family history and what illnesses you've been treated for in the past. Based on those metrics, you may not be encouraged to start training for a marathon, but you may be advised to walk a mile a day with the goal of completing that mile in twenty minutes.

A health advisor, like a financial advisor, helps you see the big picture. A wealth manager not only makes sure your portfolio is balanced among stocks, bonds, and cash so it isn't too volatile but also has the expertise to help you weather market corrections and stock dips. They can also keep you grounded against what economist Alan Greenspan has called "irrational exuberance,"[14] or when your brother-in-law tells you he can make you $500,000 in a week.

On the wellness side, an advisor will keep you from focusing on one metric and ignoring the rest. You may think you're in great shape because you work out and your BMI is under twenty, but you eat nothing but heavily processed food—everything that goes into your mouth comes from a container or the supermarket's deli—and you don't get enough sleep. The advisor will praise the diligence you show to your exercise regimen but will call your attention to the areas in which you need improvement.

Diversification in healthcare is as important as diversification in wealth. You're encouraged to keep a diversified portfolio of your financial holdings, such as different types of stocks, stable bonds, and cash. In health matters, you diversify the personnel you depend on for different wellness needs. Aside from your primary care provider and the specialists you see occasionally for specific needs, you might go for regular visits to a chiropractor, nutritionist, acupuncturist, or massage therapist, not to mention a practitioner who can help you maintain mental wellness. Depending on your primary care provider for all your medical needs is like putting all your money into mutual funds: you lose flexibility and specialized function. You're the CEO of your health, and it makes sense to delegate discrete needs to practitioners who have specialized expertise.

Advisors also track your progress. Financial counselors will keep tabs on your cash flow, how your stocks and mutual funds are doing, whether your income is rising or fluctuating, if you're amassing enough capital to fund a comfortable retirement. Doctors and other wellness counselors take similar snapshots in time, making note of blood pressure, weight, hours of sleep, nutrient consumption, frequency of exercise, and other vital metrics, while guiding them toward improvement over time.

It's important to feel that you're making progress. That doesn't mean you have to be in perfect physical shape or in perfect financial shape; it's counterproductive to set a standard for yourself that's so high you never can reach it. Dan Sullivan encouraged me to create my own scorecard. He says he sets up a game for himself so that he's always winning. One of his coaching students said that was cheating, but Dan said, "If I create it, why shouldn't I win?" And he's right. We're so used to adages such as "A man's reach should exceed his grasp" that we're always striving for perfection, but I think Dan's on to something. He's saying, if my goal is peace of mind, why wouldn't I create a game I can win all the time?

Dan and the Strategic Coach® team developed an app that I use all the time called WinStreak®.[15] Every day, it asks you for your wins—your positives. I might input that my blood pressure was in the normal range and my Ōura Ring® registered a high sleep score. It reinforces the positive things I'm doing to stay healthy.

The Balanced Wealth Approach is for everyone, not for ultra-triathletes who, let's be clear, don't need motivation. I make room for cheat days in my personal program; everybody does. If I ask an audience, "How many of you eat pizza once a month?" every hand is going to go up, starting with mine. If you're staying in good shape, you can have a cheat day once a month or so. One pizza dinner per month is not going to put you in the tomb early because you've been sticking with your program the other twenty-nine days.

The financial analogy is a client with an investment portfolio that is properly diversified and balanced who wants to take a flyer on a chancy stock. You can do that if the rest of your funds are secure or in growth position because even if the stock goes south, it isn't going to blow up your retirement. It's when you put all your funds in one area, and that market gets crushed, that you get into trouble—like the people who had all their money in tech stocks in 2000. If you stay true to your game plan, you can afford some cheat days on your diet, and you can afford some cheat days on your portfolio.

Another parallel is what happens if you don't take your counselor's advice. People who haven't done much planning come to me all the time at age fifty-five and say they want to retire in ten years. That means socking away $5,000 a month until they retire. Everything about their financial lives has to change if they're going to reach that goal.

It's similar to the guy who goes to the doctor at fifty-five in lousy shape, with poor eating and sleep habits, stressed out by the Millennials nipping at his heels on the job. The doctor, trainer, and nutritionist tell him what he has to do in order to add fifteen years to his life, and it's so overwhelming that he says, "Forget it, by then I'll be dead because everyone in my family drops dead of a heart attack by sixty-eight." He has to be convinced that no, if he turns his health habits around *now*, he'll

break the family curse and have years—happy years—
after he retires.

And there are increasing amounts of technology to
help the folks who come to health responsibility late.
Just as you can track your financial holdings on your
smartphone, you can check your blood sugar, heart rate,
and many other medical metrics on your phone. You
can buy a device that lets you get a hospital-grade EKG
reported to your phone or devices that track your fitness
levels and the amount and quality of sleep. The technology doesn't replace getting an annual checkup from your
doctor any more than it can take the place of sitting with
your financial advisor once a year, but it's ready to be
hooked up to your phone, and it provides information
daily that we used to get only when we had a physical.
Plus, there are apps such as WinStreak that serve as
motivational aids.

As you can see, there are many ways in which health
management requires an approach similar to wealth
management, which means we're at the beginning of a
time during which financial planners, properly trained,
can guide you in matters of health as well as money. That
does not mean handing off health decisions to strang-
ers any more than leaving professionals in full charge of
your finances. In both situations, you have to own your
responsibility, not outsource it to others.

I believe that right now, at this point in the twenty-
first century, we've entered a time when a great

investment firm not only will help you take care of your money but will guide you in living a healthy life that will allow you to *enjoy* your money. My business can do that now because I have knowledge of what health habits will lead you to healthy, active longevity and of comprehensive programs, such as Fountain Life or Lifeforce, that will help you get there.

Ask yourself whether you're getting that information from your financial team right now. Take a good look at them: Are you confident that your financial advisors are tuned into their own health, their own potential for long and enjoyable lives? If you aren't, maybe you need planners who understand that the most impressive portfolio in the world won't do a thing for you if you aren't alive to enjoy its fruits. The successful financial planners of the future—a future that begins right now—are the ones who bring the same mindset to make you a winner with your wealth *and* with your health.

CHAPTER 6

The Balanced Wealth Scorecard

D an Sullivan had been coaching entrepreneurs for years when he teamed up with Babs Smith. They started The Strategic Coach® Program in 1988. Since then, they and their team of coaches have coached over twenty thousand entrepreneurs in Strategic Coach, helping them to expand their entrepreneurial freedom, success, and happiness.

One of the Strategic Coach tools and processes is called the Mindset Scorecard. Participants in Strategic Coach develop their own scorecard for their clients and prospective clients to score their mindsets and measure their progress. Sullivan then developed a mechanism that's been instrumental in changing thousands more lives: a scorecard that people can use to measure in numbers their progress toward what they want to achieve.

The scorecard strategy comes from Dan's forty-plus years of experience working directly with entrepreneurs and is backed up by a long-held belief among scientists who study life goals and motivation that an endeavor worth pursuing is worth measuring. One notable example is embodied in Karl Pearson's quote in 1857 and promoted more recently by the management consultant Peter Drucker: "That which is measured, improves. That which is measured and reported, improves exponentially."

Sullivan, whose 2021 book *The Gap and the Gain* encourages people to focus on how far they've come rather than what they have yet to achieve, echoes that sentiment: "The feeling that we're making progress is powerful and positive, but it only comes from *knowing you've moved forward*, [italics mine] and the only way to know that is through specific measurements."[16] He says that "all happiness comes from measuring your progress backwards from where you are, not forwards from where you are to where you want to go." Since creating the Mindset Scorecard for Strategic Coach, Dan has written over thirty books for different aspects of success in business—ambition, time management, growth, teamwork, and many more—each containing a Mindset Scorecard by which the reader can evaluate and measure their progress. He coaches his own clients to avoid people who not only set themselves up to fail, but whose measure of success is money and status symbols. For Sullivan, success is a matter of constantly growing in self-knowledge and self-transformation. "I want the client who continually says, 'I'm frustrated now, but in three years I want to be transformed,'" he says.

Dan inspired and encouraged me to use my experiences with my own clients and develop a scorecard on the financial services aspect of my consultancy. I realized that I could get input from my own clients about how they feel about their success as well as quantifiable insights into how I feel about my clients. The scorecard allows me to compare results when I do an annual or periodic review: Where are you now compared to where you were a year or two ago? Are you comfortable with the growth of your retirement income, the amount of risk tolerance involved? Are you satisfied that our firm is shielding you from overpayment of taxes? We wanted our clients' feedback in ways that would let us know them better.

More recently, I've been applying the scorecard concept to the Balanced Wealth process. It's a no-brainer, really: clients can rank themselves in categories concerning their health that are just as important as metrics concerning their money, categories such as exercise, diet, sleep, and stress. It may be the first time that a nonmedical person has asked them these questions, but as an advisor, I know their finances intimately and know them pretty well as human beings. I can say to them, "You know, issues of health and wellness are really important in your life, and maybe you don't pay me to look after your health, but I care about you. I literally want you to live long and prosper."

So far, my clients have shown great interest in this approach. I don't want anyone to feel pressured or to think he has to open up to me about health issues just to please me, but I do want clients to understand that there's another way to think about the relationship between client and advisor. I've created my own scorecard template which includes eight categories on money matters, with clients ranking themselves on a scale of 1 to 12 in each category. Most recently I've developed a scorecard that lists the four most critical categories in financial planning and the other four in health and wellness.

The scorecard has clients rank themselves in eight categories, with the categories listed down the left-hand side of the page. From left to right, the page contains four columns, with the first column being the one containing the lowest-scored scenario and the column farthest right listing an example of a client being on top of the issue listed in the category.

Here's what we've come up with:

When we look at the first row across, which is about retirement income, the person who places themself in the first column has a long way to go and will rank themself 1, 2, or 3, depending on their degree of cluelessness. The client in the next column, ranking themself 4, 5, or 6, has checked what their Social Security benefit will be, but they're fuzzy on how much they've saved for retirement and where the accounts are. The person in the third column is planning to draw Social Security benefits at full retirement age and knows how much they have in IRAs, though they haven't formulated a plan for systematic withdrawal, so they'll rank themselves 7, 8, or 9. The person in the fourth column is going to wait to draw Social Security until they max out benefits at age seventy and know what percentage per year they'll withdraw from their savings. The difference between a rank of 10 and a rank of 12? The 10 may not have plans made yet for downsizing their lifestyle to fit within the income levels they'll face in retirement; the 12 knows exactly what they'll do.

The evaluation structure is similar in the health areas. If you take a look at the sixth row of the scorecard, which pertains to diet, you see that the score increases as you become more mindful about eating. The lowest scores say that you eat what you want, as much as you want, when you want it. There isn't an office birthday cake or a second helping you pass up, and you have no plans to eat more thoughtfully. The next column, in the 4 to 6 range, says that you have a vague sense of what a good diet is ("I really should give up red meat and eat more fruit and vegetables"), but you aren't sure how to get there. Then column 7 to 9 says you are aware of the importance of diet and how to improve it, but you don't have a systematic plan to achieve your goals. That's the person who has a salad for lunch most days and keeps

Mindset	1-3	4-6	7-9	10-12	Score
Retirement Income	The amount and source of your income in retirement are a mystery to you.	You know that you have Social Security benefits and/or a pension but you're not sure of your income beyond that.	Your plan is to use your defined benefit and Social Security funds first and will cover any shortfall by taking distributions from your accounts.	You've optimized your defined benefit and Social Security income and have a withdrawal strategy for your assets.	
Risk Tolerance	You're not sure how much risk you are comfortable taking nor the risk of your current portfolio.	You think you know the level of risk you're comfortable taking but you're not sure how risky your current portfolio is.	You know the level of risk you're comfortable with and know that your portfolio needs to be reviewed.	You have a portfolio that is commensurate with the level of risk you're comfortable taking.	
Tax Efficient	You have not considered the tax implications of your accounts.	You're aware of the tax implications but did not know anything could be done to reduce your tax liability.	You're aware of the tax implications and strategies for reducing tax liability but have not implemented any.	You're aware of the tax implications and have taken advantage of all applicable strategies.	
Investment Review	You're not sure of the last time that there was an in-depth review of your investments.	Your investment portfolio is reviewed every few years.	Your investment portfolio is reviewed at least annually.	Your investment portfolio is reviewed on a regular, systematic basis.	

Mindset	1-3	4-6	7-9	10-12	Score
Stress	You don't manage stress well and do not have a plan of attack. You are aware that stress can play a role in your health.	You have a stressful job or situation and want to reduce it, but you don't have a plan of attack.	You're aware of your stress levels and have tried to improve them, but you don't have a systematic way of monitoring and reducing your stress.	You are aware of stress levels and have a systematic plan to reduce the negative effects of stress and are constantly updating your regimen to address stress.	
Diet	You don't really focus on what you are eating and don't have any plan in place.	You have a vague sense of what a good diet is, but don't have a game plan to get there.	You are aware of the importance of diet and how to improve it, but you don't have a systematic plan.	You are aware of your diet; you have a process in place to refine and correct and make changes.	
Sleep	You don't track your sleep and you don't really focus on the quality of your sleep.	You track your sleep informally, but don't really monitor or have any mechanism to track progress.	You are aware of your sleep patterns but aren't sure how to improve them.	You are aware of your sleep patterns, and you have a process in place to monitor them.	
Exercise	You don't currently have a formal exercise plan.	You don't currently exercise but are aware of the benefits and would like to begin a process but are not sure how.	You do exercise, but because of injuries or time commitments, have not made it a regular routine in your life.	You do exercise regularly and have a game plan for modifying and adapting your workouts to your current life situation.	

628 Hebron Avenue | Building 2, Suite 216 | Glastonbury, CT 06033 | 860.659.8200
195 Danbury Road | Suite 100 | Wilton, CT 06897 | 203.563.0665
www.capitalwm.com | info@capitalwm.com
Securities and advisory services offered through Commonwealth Financial Network, Member FINRA/SIPC, a Registered Investment Adviser. Fixed insurance products and services offered through Capital Wealth Management, LLC or CES Insurance Agency.

the dressing on the side but who suspends any rules for dinners, banquets, and buffets. People in the fourth category are aware of what they eat, consume only what they need when they need to, and have a process in place to refine and correct their food intake.

Of course, for the scorecard to be put to useful purpose, people need to be honest with themselves and not bump up their scores past reality. Let's face it, everyone wants to have a high score, and some folks are not past stretching the truth to get one. My strong recommendation is to add some outside, objective resource to verify and track your results. For example, my Ōura ring is my outside source for my sleep and exercise scores. My periodic blood draws are the source that verify my supplements such as Vitamin D are in a normal range. One example of stretching the truth might be the person who wants a high rank in the exercise category and says, "Yes, I have a formal exercise routine" when that "routine" is simply walking the dog down the block and back. Is it a routine? Yes. Does it involve exercise? Sure. Is it an hour of Pilates? Not even close. (And bending down to pick up dog poop isn't "stretching" either.) To see these charts online, visit www.thebalancedwealthapproach.com.

When I get the results from the scorecard, I sit down with the client, review the numbers with them, and ask what they think about it in an open, nonjudgmental way. That usually elicits a response on the spectrum from thrilled, to happy, to "meh," to unhappy, to devastated.

Then my task is to keep them engaged in future steps, whether on money or health. Over the next few weeks, I'll find out whether the clients are motivated to raise their scores, assuming they're lower than the clients expected or lower than what's optimal for their well-being.

The top score is 96 (eight categories times twelve rating levels), and people with a high score will often ask how to maintain it, especially if their circumstances are about to change, such as an impending retirement or plans to sell the family home. Those with lower numbers have a variety of responses: "I didn't know that"; "I don't have time to keep track of details"; "I don't have a system." The biggest difference is between the people who want to improve their scores and the people who say, "I know I could do better, but I'm not interested." Even with people who aren't highly motivated to raise their scores, I can ask if there's anything they want to focus on. There might be things I discover I can tweak on the financial side, which I can then run by them.

If the score isn't where they want it to be, clients need to *want* to put in the effort so they can move to the next level, and they need to be patient while they wait for it to work. That might mean that we recommend a nutritionist or a physical therapist, help coordinate a sleep study, and/or find accountability partners for some of our clients. We also have to decide where we stand with clients who *aren't* interested in moving forward with a health and wellness regimen, and we need to always remember that life is not static. Things happen to us, good and bad, that change our routines. With the first round of the Balanced Wealth scorecard, we hope to find the same degree of honesty and clarity we ask of our clients about financial issues and an idea of what the client wants to do with the information they receive from the scorecard.

At some point, I may develop a scorecard solely devoted to wellness, but I don't want to overwhelm people, scare them, or make them feel guilty. I want to keep the scorecard simple so everyone can see a victory for themselves somewhere. That's when clients acknowledge and choose to change their behavior in any one of the categories and there's a mechanism to measure their progress. I have a loose definition of "victory": if someone starts taking sensible supplements and reads a book or two about a health problem, I consider that a victory—a step in the right direction. Remember, the journey of a thousand miles begins with a single step.

Stress is going to be a very important part of the scorecard. There's been a lot of research done on stress in recent years, and we know now that it's a contributor to dozens of medical maladies—certainly heart trouble and even cancer. Chronic high levels of the stress hormone cortisol can make someone sick at any age. There's been a flood of writing about how stressed high school students are, but stress management isn't part of the usual high school curriculum, even in health classes or physical education.

If kids are given any guidance at all about stress management, it's stuff they see as meaningless recommendations, such as "Get enough sleep," "Think in positive terms," and "Remember every situation is temporary." I don't know what's worse—not having *any* guidance on staying healthy, which was the case for our generation, or the platitudes and clichés teenagers get today. At least many schools now counsel kids about diet and exercise.

We know there's such a thing as *good* stress; that's what motivates you to get up in the morning and make things happen. If you have no stress in your life at all—no need to earn a living, no responsibilities, no one ever judging you—then everything slides off you and nothing affects you. That sounds less like a privilege and more like a wall between you and any number of pleasurable pursuits, such as being in a loving relationship or doing something creative.

But *bad* stress, past the point of what you expect or can handle, really has an effect on your well-being. I know people from martial arts who train regularly, exercise a lot, keep themselves very fit, and have excellent eating habits. But they start graying early, or they look worn out and older than they are. That, I think, is due to stress.

A person who signs up for a comprehensive program such as Health Nucleus or Fountain Life has access to tests for compounds in the human body that are heightened by stress and can find strategies for bringing them down. One is high-sensitivity C-reactive protein (hs-CRP), a marker for inflammation that can predict a number of serious cardiovascular diseases. When someone has fought off an illness, has a fever or infection, or has suffered tissue damage, hs-CRP is often raised.

Another is homocysteine, an amino acid and natural by-product of cellular metabolism, which vitamins B_{12}, B_6, and folate generally break down in the body to keep normal levels very low. Too much homocysteine can damage blood vessels and lead to blood clots, so heightened homocysteine count has been associated with dementia and heart disease. Stress is linked to inflammation, which in turn is identified with a vast array of reasons for health issues, and people with elevated levels of homocysteine are often experiencing deficiencies of the B vitamins listed here.

There are many short- and long-term strategies for reducing stress. Proven or effective techniques include various breathing exercises, aromatherapy, massage, steam or sauna treatment, listening to a favorite piece of music, and watching something that provokes laughter. Ongoing activities such as meditation, yoga, regular workouts, and even work and workspace organization have reduced stress as well. The scientist Jon Kabat-Zinn, trained as a molecular biologist, created a career for himself in stress management after studying with a Zen Buddhist teacher during graduate school. He placed Buddhist tenets in a secular framework and promoted them as an effective way to bring down stress. Others have made progress in stress management studying what happens when perceived ability to handle a situation doesn't match up with the situation itself.

I believe financial advisors are empowered to ask our clients questions about stress, to suggest strategies for handling stress (which is not the same as giving medical advice), and to send them back to their doctors armed with the vocabulary needed to ask for specific medical opinions on stress management. When patients do that, physicians are not only able to give them more help but are reminded of techniques they can use themselves.

My massage therapist has an entire sub-practice based on doctors. One surgeon liked her work—and the fact that she knew her muscle groups thoroughly—and referred her to several colleagues who also benefited from her ministrations. It's amazing how few physicians, whose work can be very stressful depending on specialty and workload, pursue stress management. Their situation is analogous to the shoemaker's children who go without shoes. Physicians should be the first to understand how to employ anti-stress strategies, but many don't do so.

If you look again at strategies for stress management, you'll see some diagnostics and therapies that can get expensive, but many others cost little or nothing—and it doesn't cost extra to ask a doctor about them. By reducing your stress, you can diminish many of the aches, pains, and illnesses of a hectic life. You may even make them disappear.

Expanding my wealth management practice to include issues of health and wellness isn't just about the potential to attract more clients and earn more money—it's also about my own health and wellness. Frankly, I enjoy working with clients who are also mindful of, or ready to be mindful of, their personal health. There have been times when I've avoided buying a business that could make money for me because dealing with the owner of that business would have put more stress in my life than I wanted. I can honestly say I've turned away from financial gain when I looked at a situation and said, "You know what? This is not going to enhance my health regimen." In that way, my focus on health has helped me filter out misguided career moves.

This focus on health also has allowed me to explore with my clients a range of subjects they never brought up before. When a client is comfortable sharing those discussions with me, our conversations are deeper and more meaningful, and I think it creates a more robust picture of what I'm offering them as a planner. As I work with more and more clients using the Balanced Wealth approach, I become more convinced that these parallel tracks of wealth and health allow people to make more stable, well-reasoned decisions about their futures. At this point, there is no other way I would want to live my life except to know the metrics, and the scorecard is one of the most effective ways to discover them.

CHAPTER 7

Precision Medicine: "Don't Die of Something Stupid!"

We don't really have a healthcare system, despite what you've heard. In fact, we have a sick-care system. You get sick, you go to the doctor; the sicker you are, the more lucrative it is for the people in the healthcare system. The doctor tries their best, and you either get well or you don't. In any case, you or your insurance company pays up.

That's how it works, and that's not very good.

The problem is that most serious illnesses, such as cancer, heart disease, memory disorders, and other brain-related illnesses, do not become evident until it's too late to treat them. A person goes to a doctor complaining of chest pain, shortness of breath, or headaches. Tests reveal lung disease, blocked arteries, or brain tumors, but by the time they cause physical pain, they're all but impossible to treat. A possible answer is chemotherapy, which has varying success rates and has many side effects, or heart surgery, which is also risky. The result is early death. Worse, it's preventable death.

Take the case of Chadwick Boseman, the star of the successful movie *Black Panther*. He died of colon cancer at age forty-three. Why was his cancer undetected until it reached a point where it was inoperable? Because doctors recommend today that people only start getting colonoscopies at age forty-five. The problem is that Chadwick Boseman was not a statistic. He was a human being. What if he had undergone a colonoscopy at an earlier age? The simple answer is that he might very well be alive today, healthy, living his life, and starring in more movies.

There are tens or even hundreds of millions of Chadwick Bosemans out there, people who are seemingly destined to die before their time because serious and lethal medical conditions were not identified when they still could have been treated. Advances in detection, including sequencing our genomes, have made it possible for a select few to discover whether they are candidates for such fatal illnesses; these lucky individuals are able to discover these conditions years or even decades before they become fatal. As a result, they are able to get treatment for what are currently precursors to cancer, heart disease, brain issues, or other critical and severe illnesses while the treatment is still simple, manageable, low-risk, and low-cost.

So the simple question is this: Why aren't you one of those people?

If you are not in this favored group, it's simply because you are not a member of a "precision medicine" practice, for example, Human Longevity on the West Coast and Fountain Life based in New York and Atlanta. These places perform an incredibly deep dive into your health-care status, including sequencing your own genome. As a result, they are able to identify healthcare issues long before those issues develop into fatal illnesses. Of course, there are many other precision medicine clinics around the country that you can and should investigate to determine which is the best fit for you.

These medical groups accomplish this mission, which sounds like something out of science fiction, by using cutting-edge tools and technologies to survey every aspect of your health from top to bottom. At both places, you will undergo a brain and full-body MRI, a CT scan of the heart, a heart ultrasound, and extensive bloodwork. In addition, Human Longevity provides clients with a whole genome sequencing report as well as additional tests including wearables. The result is an incomparably complete picture of the state of your health, which lets you and your doctors know whether there's anything concerning that needs to be addressed or watched immediately as well as what your risks are for future chronic age-related disease.

What do Human Longevity and Fountain Life have in common? They have Peter Diamandis, founder of the XPRIZE Foundation, author of *Abundance: The Future Is Better Than You Think* and other books, and an M.D. who has dedicated his life to discovering new ways to create health and wellness for everyone. Diamandis speaks to the concept called "longevity escape velocity." The idea is that for every year you live, science discovers a new way to add a year to your life. If you do your part—taking care of your diet, exercising, including enough rest, and managing stress—in theory, you could live forever. That's because science is busily creating new ways to extend life. Longevity escape velocity may seem like a fantasy today, but it's just around the corner. Indeed, scientists who study these matters say that the first person to live to 150 has already been born. Perhaps it's one of your grandchildren!

The goal both at Human Longevity and Fountain Life is to get members past the century mark—to live to one hundred and beyond. But as Dr. Bill Kapp, CEO of Fountain Life, says, "Nobody wants to live to 110 if they're biologically 110 years old! Wouldn't you rather live to 110 with the body of a fifty-year-old? That's what we deliver. Longevity plus fantastic health. That's what our members enjoy."

Here's another example, this one from Fountain Life. Everybody knows that plaque sticks to and narrows the walls of our arteries, depending on our diets and exercise choices, genetics, and other factors. A sign of plaque buildup is the amount of calcium in your arteries, which can be measured by a CT scan, but that doesn't give you all the results. The question, then, becomes even if you measure your plaque, how much of it is "good" plaque, which doesn't affect health, and how much is "bad" plaque, which can break off and travel to occlude a blood vessel completely? That can lead to fatal heart attacks even for people in their forties. I passed this test with flying colors, but I still get checked regularly because of my family's medical history. None of us can afford to take any of these things for granted.

The testing regimen at Fountain Life allows people to learn not just how much plaque they have but how much of it is the dangerous kind. As a result, different people with the same total level of plaque will have different treatment paths, depending on how much of that plaque is lethal and how much is benign. Wouldn't you want to know your own scores right now instead of waiting for a heart attack to take you out of the game? After all, as I said at the outset of this book, what good is a seven-figure portfolio if you're six feet under?

It's not just about having the information regarding the state of affairs inside your heart, lungs, colon, kidneys, brain, and other vital organs. It's also knowing what to do about it. Fountain Life, Lifeforce, and Human Longevity are light-years ahead of most other "executive check-up" institutions, even the ones with the big brand names you may have heard of or even visited. Not only do Fountain Life and Human Longevity have the cutting-edge tools for analysis and detection, but they also have access to medications and treatment pathways that may be underutilized by your local general practitioner.

In fact, because a precision medical platform is not restricted by the rules of insurance companies, it can tailor diagnostic and therapeutic measures to an individual patient. I'm sure you've heard many stories of patients whose doctors knew what test the patient needed but couldn't get it for that patient because their insurance company required that tests be done in a certain order. Or the doctor knew which medicine would best treat the patient's condition, but the insurers insisted that another drug be administered first, and only when that one failed would they approve the medication the doctor wanted. A precision medical practice will also determine which method of testing provides the most accurate results—sometimes a method less invasive than what is usually done—rather than adopting a "one size fits all" approach.

Right now, the kind of healthcare analysis we're talking about in these pages is available to anyone willing and able to write a substantial check. The annual fees and/or service models for Health Nucleus can be found at www.humanlongevity.com, and for Fountain Life you can visit www.FountainLife.com. But it's very likely that within ten years, the approach that Fountain Life and Human Longevity are pioneering will become the standard of healthcare for everyone. How can I make such a bold claim? It's simple—the costs of technology and testing are constantly dropping. The best analogy I can provide is that of electric cars. A generation ago, cars that ran on batteries sounded like something out of a science fiction movie. Then along came Tesla, whose first car cost as much as $300,000. Then the cost of batteries went down because there was so much competition in the world of batteries. As a result, the Chevy Volt came along, the Toyota Prius came along, and so did several lower-priced lines of Tesla. Today a battery-powered car is pretty much a possibility for even a moderately affluent person in our society.

The same thing is going to happen to the costs of medical analysis. Right now, every patient who goes through a Human Longevity or a Fountain Life exam is benefiting from tests that—if taken separately in the traditional current medical system—can cost more than the annual price offered per patient. They are banking on the fact that the costs of testing will continue to drop precipitously over the next few years. Powerful equipment such as MRI scanners has been coming down in price as has the price of whole genome sequencing.

There are two reasons why the cost of testing will drop in amazing ways. First, many of the fees that go into analyzing the data are paid to doctors. Their role in data analysis will be in part swept to the side by artificial intelligence, a process that has already begun. Second, the more competition there is in any technology space, the more the prices drop. So before long, we will see the cost of sequencing an entire genome to drop from over $2,000, where it is today, to a few dollars—just the cost of the electricity necessary to run the tests!

That's why I say with confidence that even though Human Longevity and Fountain Life are really for the elite (and that includes you, dear reader!), their work is leading to the democratization of healthcare in the world. They are not just democratizing healthcare; they are moving us from the sick-care standard I mentioned at the outset of this chapter to a system that really measures health and does so for everyone in the world.

The Executive Chairman of Human Longevity, Dr. Wei-Wu He, describes Human Longevity today as a five-star-level healthcare provider. In ten years, Dr. He says, instead of being a company that charges Ritz-Carlton–level pricing, it will be more like a Starbucks—a data collection point for everyone in society using AI to help derive health insights from the data. So what Human Longevity and Fountain Life are providing today to affluent consumers is actually the foundation of what companies will be providing to everyone on the planet a decade from now. And when that happens, we will see lower healthcare costs, considerably better outcomes, and a world where people don't have to "die of something stupid," as one of Human Longevity's team members likes to say.

There's absolutely no point in being the richest guy in the cemetery, wouldn't you agree?

CHAPTER 8

What Does It Take to Motivate Someone to Wellness?

Let's say I have a client who's a successful lawyer/executive/business owner in his late fifties or early sixties. He isn't an athlete, but he's no couch potato either. He plays golf and has a stationary bike at home that he actually uses. He loves good food and a glass of wine to go with it. Who wouldn't? Since he feels OK, he has a routine physical every year and doesn't feel the need to pay a lot of attention to health metrics.

I would say to him, "You know, you're working so hard to accumulate money. Don't you want to be around to spend it? I see too many clients your age die before their life expectancy." Yes, I'm his investment guy, but I feel that I get to have this conversation with him. After all, he's entrusted me to help build his future; I figure it's OK for me at least to try to help make sure he *has* a future.

Some people can turn themselves around on a dime. They get up one morning, look at themselves in the mirror, and say, "No more. The weight loss starts right now." They completely change their eating and drinking habits *that day.* Six months later, they've lost fifty pounds and seven inches around the waist, and they're running 10K races.

Not my client. After I first speak to him about his health—noting that he does get some exercise and asking if he has eating habits he could revise—he might make some progress on his own, but he doesn't have a plan. One day a week, he may get a salad for lunch instead of a cheesesteak. Once a month, he may skip the birthday cake in the conference room. That's a start, but I want my client to have a real plan, to know what he's going to eat before he eats it. I sell it on the basis of control: What you eat is something you can control. Since a lot of my successful clients like to be in control, that kind of thinking makes sense to them.

It's the same thing with sleep. Dozens of books and articles have called seven to eight hours of restful sleep a "wonder drug." One book listed a series of health benefits and asked, "If you could get all these benefits from a drug, wouldn't everyone be taking it?"[17] Of course, that "drug" is good sleep, and the author goes on to explain the science behind the health benefits.

I can then advise a client *how* to get better sleep: no electronic screens just before sleep; no meals after early evening; set a fixed time for bedtime; avoid light pollution. Anyone who can control eating habits can control sleep habits, especially if you use the "scared straight" approach and warn that lack of restful sleep over the years puts a person at greater risk for dementia. Sleep clears out the gunk in your brain that turns into amyloid plaques, the telltale mark of Alzheimer's disease. Don't you want to be able to recognize your kids and your grandchildren twenty years from now? Don't you want to be able to keep up hobbies, visit friends, and travel?

In fact, Dr. Rudolph Tanzi, professor of neurology at Harvard Medical School and codirector of the McCance Center for Brain Health at Massachusetts General Hospital, has an acronym for an overall health program that can ward off dementia. He calls it SHIELD:

- **S**leep
- **H**andling stress
- **I**nteracting with others
- **E**xercise
- **L**earning new things
- **D**iet[18]

Poor sleep is also a factor in heart disease, diabetes, depression, and other maladies. That's why so many people have been using wearable sleep trackers, some as small as wedding bands, that measure your movement and other metrics such as heart rate to log your sleep duration, sleep stages, and the number of times you awaken at night. Some are so sensitive that their accuracy rivals that of an overnight sleep study in a hospital.

My main objective in inviting clients to fill out health items on a scorecard and discuss their health habits with me is to present their challenges with possible solutions. Folks come to me with a list of problems that are making them depressed, and I'd like to be able to help them find the path to lighten their load. The motivational speaker and author Tony Robbins has long insisted that if you can find a big enough *why*, you'll always find a *how*. The key word, of course, is *motivation*.

Here's a golden oldie:

Q: How many therapists does it take to change a lightbulb?
A: Only one, but the lightbulb really has to *want* to change.

Changing habits—any habits—requires motivation. It isn't enough to *wish* that you were thinner, more athletic, or quicker to fall asleep. It isn't even enough to *want* those things. Motivation is what makes you want so much to change your habits that you're willing to do things you don't like, even suffer, in order to make the change happen.

What does motivation look like? Is it avoiding Alzheimer's? Is it the Disney cruise with the grandchildren?

Is it getting rid of a few aches and pains, or is it being able to do things you did thirty years ago? It has to be something strong because motivation to change health habits is hard to come by. Ice cream tastes better than broccoli. The gym is boring. Sitting is easier than exercising. People already know the path they're on now is killing them.

I'd say one motivation is being able to enjoy the wealth later in life that they're building now. That's the theme of this book, really, that you have to be the CEO of your own health. I know I've said it before, but a lot of people need to hear it again and again: unless you take action to improve your health now, you aren't going to enjoy that money after you retire, and neither will anyone you love. You want to be alert and ambulatory. You want to check off the items on your bucket list. You want to use your money on a trip to Iceland in June and Rio de Janeiro in February and to help put your grandkids through college; you don't want your money to get sucked up by the costs of nursing homes and hospitals.

Related to that is the desire to be with your family in an active way as long as possible. I turned thirty-six the year my daughter was born and was in my early forties when my son came along, so if I want to have an active role in the lives of *their* children—if indeed, they are blessed with children—I need to live a long and healthy life. So a second motivator might be a client's wish to become a patriarch or matriarch, to look lovingly over three generations of descendants.

Yet another motivator isn't as pleasant to contemplate, but it involves visualizing what the end of your life will be like. We hear often of a "good death" when someone dies in her sleep, without suffering, her heart giving out deep into old age, after a busy day and a good dinner. That isn't the way death comes for most people. They spend their last days bedridden, hooked up to IVs and ventilators. The COVID-19 pandemic brought home to many of us how frightening it is to die struggling for air and how traumatizing it is to witness that kind of death. If people are really unlucky, the last two or three years of their lives are spent on dialysis or in rounds of chemotherapy or tethered to oxygen tanks. Or, maybe worse, your brain function shrinks before your body gives out, and your loved ones lose you years before you're gone.

It's the "scared straight" approach again: Is this the death you want for yourself—a long, painful decline culminating in the confusion and struggle of a hospital room? And for this to happen in your sixties or seventies when you should still have many active years ahead of you? Do you want the money you worked so hard to accumulate to be siphoned off to pay medical bills? To spend your time at doctors' appointments and hospital stays instead of playing with your grandchildren? To become a burden on the family you love and who loves you? What if I told you that if you take care of yourself now, years and years from now you'll have that good death?

There's this consideration too: if you pay attention to your health now, you'll be perceived as someone who's ahead of the curve, who thinks ahead when other people attend only to the status quo.

I'll quote Joyce Sunada once again: "If you don't make time for your wellness, you will be forced to make time for your illness." She learned this lesson the hard way when she had to take a medical leave from teaching. A lot of people don't give a thought to their health until something happens to them and they go into crisis mode—a condition not conducive to thinking straight.

But the best time to think about your health is when you're *not* fighting disease. As John F. Kennedy said, "The best time to repair the roof is when the sun is shining."[19] You want to get your health habits under control before you get sick, because it will be ten times more difficult to do it during or after a serious illness.

Ben Horowitz, who started a venture capital firm with Netscape founder Marc Andreessen, once said that business leaders can be either wartime CEOs—beleaguered captains who are hunkered down trying to save the company—or peacetime CEOs, who have the opportunity to pursue innovation and expand the business.[20] If you transfer this idea to health, the wartime

CEO is the person fighting cancer or heart disease or liver malfunction, while the peacetime CEO is trying new ways to strengthen himself and lessen his chances of getting sick. If nothing else, the peacetime CEO is having more fun!

Also, if your doctors see that you're going above and beyond in terms of maintaining your health, those doctors are going to go the extra mile for you. Healthcare personnel love a model patient; it makes things so much easier for them.

Doctors get frustrated by patients who don't cooperate, who have no interest in their own wellness, and/ or who are hostile to the doctor's instructions. Some patients are fatalistic and don't think anything the doctor says or does will work; others act as if the doctor should be able to fix whatever problem they have, simply because the doctor is the professional, and that's what a professional is paid to do. It's like expecting a plumber to fix a toilet in five minutes even though your two-year-old shoved a newspaper and three rubber duckies in it.

By contrast, the patient who knows he is his own primary healthcare provider and is operating as a partner with his doctor is going to get more personal attention and possibly better care. You can show the doctor that you aren't about to offload your healthcare to him, expecting him to work miracles on your behalf. To sum up, here are some immediate, simple, free, and easy steps you can take right now to improve your sense of well-being.

Sleep

- Go to bed at about the same time every night.
- Sleep in a cool room. The American Sleep Association recommends no more than 68 degrees Fahrenheit, but make it as cool as you find tolerable.
- Turn off devices using blue light (i.e., screens) an hour before bedtime.
- Don't eat within three hours of going to bed. If you must eat later, make it something light, because a heavy meal will affect the digestive *and* sleep cycle.
- Stay away from caffeine after 3:00 p.m.
- Alcohol will put you to sleep, but you won't sleep well. Try not to drink alcohol close to bedtime.[21]

Diet

- Follow the Mediterranean diet, which is high in fruits, vegetables, legumes, fish, and nuts.[22]
- Make the next meal you eat a little healthier than the previous one was. For example, if your next meal is breakfast and you like oatmeal, have it with blueberries instead of sugar, and cut down the extra fat (butter or milk).
- Once you're eating one healthy meal a day, try for a full day of healthy meals. Then see how many healthy-eating days you can rack up in a row.

- Keep your salads all-veggie and your dressings on the side.
- Monitor your intake of sugar and salt. Salt raises blood pressure, and sugar can help cause gut inflammation, feeding bad bacteria in your digestive tract.
- Allow yourself a small "naughty treat" once in a while.
- The Internet has dozens of "healthy eating" sites operated by nonprofits and government agencies that have no sales agenda. They offer many tips for changing and maintaining your diet as there are also many variations of the Mediterranean diet to suit your preferences and make it more sustainable.[23]

Exercise

- Walk a half-mile, moving up gradually to a mile and more, every day. Recent data has demonstrated a short walk, even as brief as ten minutes, post-meals can substantially improve cardiovascular and metabolic health.
- Make time to be outdoors when it's sunny for at least ten minutes a day to activate vitamin D.
- Stretch your arms, back, torso, and legs every morning.

- Use the Internet to research the best exercise programs for your age and for the level of stamina you have when you begin. But expect it to increase in time![24]

Stress

- Learn some breathing techniques for a quick slowdown.
- Go outside and enjoy nature whenever you can.
- Try not to "sweat the small stuff."
- Express your stress by sharing it with a close friend or relative or writing in a journal.
- If it's appropriate for you, find a good therapist who can objectively look at your situation and give valuable feedback and solutions you might not have thought of.[25]
- Smile more! Clinical neuroscientist Dr. Philip DeFina, Ph.D., whom I recently saw for a brain scan, told me smiling and hydration should be as big of a priority as diet, sleep, exercise, and stress reduction. So seek out funny books, movies, and TV shows. Laughter is great medicine!

And here's one more motivator: many people resist steps to improve their wellness by saying, "You know what? That tense, chubby couch potato scarfing chips and playing video games half the night? That's the real me. That's just who I am, and I accept the consequences." But what if that *isn't* the real you? Maybe the *real* you is forty pounds lighter, gets eight hours of sleep every night, can touch his toes, and doesn't let setbacks get to him? And what if the real you actually wants to live a few years (or a decade) longer than the couch-potato you?

Just think about it. You're the CEO of your own health. Take control, monitor your progress, and move forward. Today.

CHAPTER 9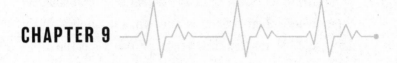

Tracking Your Progress in Health and Wealth

Clients of financial planners always should keep track of what's happening with their money. We planners certainly keep track of it, and we send our clients regular statements of how their accounts are doing. Some clients are content to know the nest egg they invested with us has grown and is keeping up with inflation, so they just look at the raw total. If someone invested $1 million through me and it appreciated to $2 million over the next seven years, net of fees, we would be thrilled knowing this is a great rate of return for a growth portfolio.

Another client, more risk-averse, might be happy to have that same $1 million be worth $1.5 million in seven years. The rate of return may not be as high, but it runs well ahead of historical inflation. I may have to reassure this client that the risks he's taking are worth taking even if the stock market is volatile or inflation spikes, but as long as the money is growing, the client is OK.

Other clients prefer a lot of detailed information about where their money is and what it's doing. They may ask, "What's the rate of return? What has the inflation rate done to my total holdings since I first invested with you? Since this time last year? What's the rate of growth in my mutual funds compared to how the different indexes in the stock market are doing? Do I need more diversification? How am I being protected against emergencies?" These clients will want more specifics if they're nervous about volatility or inflation, but they're also more likely to know that volatility in the stock market is cyclical but normal and that conditions such as inflation are temporary.

Either type of client wants to know three basic things about their money:

- Am I better off having invested with you versus just leaving my money in a bank?
- Are you doing a better job of growing my funds than another planner would do?
- Did you prevent me from investing my money poorly?

When you translate those three questions into health language, you get these:

- Is it necessary for me to consult health practitioners if I'm feeling OK and don't have a lot of wellness concerns?
- If I do go to a doctor, is one any better than another?
- Did the steps I took prevent me from making a huge health mistake?

It's amazing how many people think this way, not shopping around for the best practitioners to meet their needs, tracking their money more than they do their health. People will consult experts when anything comes up in their financial lives: They got a new job. They remarried someone with kids and are now expecting a baby of their own. They just inherited some money. Their daughter is getting married next year, and they need to save up for her wedding. These and a thousand other scenarios are situations in which someone will want to consult an expert and say, "Excuse me, I need to make an adjustment to my risk profile."

I'd like people to think about their health with the same attention to changing situations and conditions. You can be fine, but suddenly you could slip and fall. Did you break something? Did you pull a muscle? If you broke your wrist, that could be a trip to the emergency room, a cast, instructions, and physical therapy. Even if you just pulled a muscle, you have to take some immediate steps to alleviate the pain and promote healing—rest, apply ice and heat, see if you can work out the pain, and check how you feel the next day. A broken wrist brings a certain set of problems to your work life and daily life; there will be things you can't do, at least for a few weeks, and you'll figure out workarounds while you heal. Still, the pulled muscle can be instructive too. How does it affect my movement? My motivation? How can I prevent it in the future? These are questions people need to ask to get themselves closer to their fitness goals.

I want people to set a standard of waking up every day feeling *excellent,* not just good or OK. If you have *excellent* as your baseline, you'll ask questions about why you don't feel *excellent* when you don't. I have many days where I don't wake up feeling *excellent*; I may feel *good,* but that doesn't keep me from trying to attain *excellent.* My sleep score might be down because I have jet lag from a trip, or maybe a few late-night meals kept me from REM sleep. Either way, I want to have a game plan to get back to *excellent.* If you strive for *excellent* and miss it, you end up at *good.* If you strive for *good* or *OK,* you might end up at *meh* or even *crummy.*

It's important not to compare your physical condition to that of other people. As President Theodore Roosevelt once said, "Comparison is the thief of joy." Why compare yourself to an NBA power forward or an NFL linebacker? They've had years of training and conditioning that you didn't have as well as possible innate advantages. We can learn from their regimens, but we're unlikely to be able to eat and exercise at their level. (Wait until they retire; some ex-athletes may wind up comparing themselves to *you*.) You don't want to compare your physical progress to anybody's but yours.

And even if we don't compare ourselves to impossible standards, we all have egos and want to think we're hitting all our health targets. When the program I use shares my health numbers, I score above average in many categories, but I'm below average in others. My competitive nature says, *Whoa!* After that moment of disbelief, though, those are the categories that get my attention, and I concentrate on improving those areas. Six months or a year later, when I see progress in categories that used to be substandard, I get an extra boost from being better off than I was earlier. That's why Dan Sullivan's advice is so good: don't focus on the shortfall; focus on what you've gained since the day you started.

Tracking allows you to make improvements, and it shows you where your regimen needs to change. Life doesn't stay the same, and neither do you. So you want to keep adjusting your wellness practices to suit where you are at the moment. This can happen to a large group; for example, a few years ago, coaches began to test college athletes for vitamin D intake in the face of lower performance, and they found that most of their players were deficient—if not in the vitamin itself, then in its activation by sunlight. They established a regimen by which students were assured sufficient vitamin D and the outdoor time to activate it.

When you track any facet of your life and see gain, it increases your confidence level and confirms that the path you're on is the correct one. It also works to improve motivation. Let's say you work with my Balanced Wealth scorecard for six months, and after those months you've become more mindful of your sleep habits, diet, and exercise routine. You may not have made big changes in those areas, but you know a lot more about them now and are ready and willing to put that knowledge into practice.

I wanted to improve my sleep habits, so I bought an Oura Ring®, a top-of-the-line sleep tracker that provides information I needed for this purpose. I was pleased to receive an initial score of 82 (out of 100), and my goal became to reach 90. Setting a goal that was a little further away than the present reality gave me a reason—motivation—for doing what I needed to do to get more restful sleep.

By nature, I think we humans are wired to compare ourselves to standards or to people we admire; we're also wired to move forward from where we are, but we need motivation for forging that forward path. These beliefs of mine can be applied to health issues as easily as to financial planning, and if people are willing to keep track of the elements of each system, to take measurements and keep their noses out of other people's business, they can make great strides in both.

Just as people need motivation to change their behaviors, they need motivation to keep track of them in detail. They need to be reminded that if you don't track your health, you won't get to enjoy the money you've earned. Your life at the end will be measured in DALYs (Disability-Adjusted Life Years): years lost to disability. Who wants to wake up every morning with back pain, anxiety, sore joints, or worse? Once you've done the hard part, accumulating the money you need for retirement, it only makes sense to be able to enjoy the years afterward.

I don't look at new behaviors or tracking them as a burden or something you lose. Going on a hike may not be something you thought of doing before age sixty, but the scenery is a lot prettier than the view at the fitness center. Having salmon with a side of green beans for dinner isn't necessarily less tasty than a sixteen-ounce Porterhouse steak and a loaded baked potato; it's just different. And once you get used to keeping a record of what you eat, it'll become second nature, and you won't even think about it. "Not comparing" also means not comparing your behaviors now to what your life was like before. There's only moving forward.

What should we track, and how?

Start with the low-hanging fruit, the easiest activities to measure and record.

Wearable devices have made it effortless to track both sleep patterns and many fitness activities. Trackers that go around your wrist or finger can tell you how long you slept during the night, the amount of time you spent in REM (deep, dream-state) sleep, how restorative your sleep was, your blood's oxygen level, your heart rate, your body temperature, and many other details not only about your sleep but also how that sleep affects you during the day.

Devices such as Apple Watch and Fitbit can record the number of steps you take during the day, how fast you walk or run and how far, and vital signs such as heart rate and oxygen saturation (more sophisticated models present a real-time electrocardiogram); some even can warn of atrial fibrillation, an irregular heart rhythm. Recent devices measure the body's reaction to stress and offer instruction on mindfulness and stress reduction. And—get ready, tech lovers—at least one company is working on the software to aggregate data from Fitbit, Apple Watch, and Oura Ring®.

You can keep track of what you eat by maintaining a food diary on paper or in your smartphone, going over it later to check for unhealthy fats, excess carbohydrates and sugars, and overconsumption of calories. It doesn't advocate for one diet over another or scold you for slipping up; it just makes you mindful of what you swallow.

Depending on how detailed and organized your food diary is—the more, the better—you'll find out a lot about what you eat and why you feel the way you do when you eat it. Sodium (salt) intake is a big factor for many people because of its link to high blood pressure, and other people have sensitivities to sodium outside blood pressure concerns.

For example, a few years ago, I noticed that whenever I traveled, my breathing would become a bit labored, and I would need to use my asthma spray a lot more. I couldn't figure it out until I read a guide from the American Heart Association that said people with asthma are sensitive to sodium; consume too much and you'll experience the symptoms of a mild asthma attack. When you travel, you eat a lot of prepackaged and restaurant-prepared food containing much more salt than the food you prepare at home.

Sodium that is present naturally in fresh foods usually isn't the problem, with the exception of some cheese and seafood. (Most fresh fruits and vegetables are very low in sodium; exceptions include spinach and Swiss chard, the sodium content of which means you don't have to sprinkle salt on them. The same applies to many fresh protein sources.) The trouble comes from foods that have salt added to them in the form of brine, preservatives, and flavor enhancement, such as deli meats, condiments, breakfast cereal (that's right), breads, frozen meals, vegetable juices, prepared sauces and gravies, and pretty much anything in a can. *Most processed foods from the grocery store and dishes served in restaurants are loaded with added salt.*

Sugar is another common additive, appearing in many processed foods that we don't think of as sweet, such as ketchup, spaghetti sauce, barbecue sauce, canned soups, and canned vegetables. It's also added in quantity to many products we think are good for us, such as yogurt, sports drinks, fruit juices, protein bars, and breakfast cereals. A startling number of breakfast cereals contain more sugar than grain by weight! No matter what it's called in the list of ingredients, any natural sweetener, dry or syrup, contains four grams of sugar per teaspoon, and it doesn't take many teaspoons to meet maximum daily recommendations.

Excessive sugar intake, of course, is associated with type 2 diabetes. A type 2 diabetic person's body is resistant to the amount of insulin its pancreas produces, and when the pancreas can't produce enough insulin to keep up with the sugar someone consumes (or creates by overconsumption of carbohydrates), the amount of glucose in the blood rises. Accordingly, people who develop type 2 diabetes need to decrease their intake of sugars and carbs.

Sugar also plays a role in the activity of *H. pylori*, a common stomach bacterium that causes inflammation in the upper digestive tract. It's responsible in small amounts for maladies such as upset stomach and acid reflux and in large amounts for ulcers and as a precursor to stomach cancer. It's also associated with higher levels of the biomarker for blood sugar and diabetes. I found out about this connection when a test showed a small amount of *H. pylori* in my system. It was small enough to be knocked out with antibiotics, and once it was gone, I stopped having minor acid reflux and was able to eat dinner an hour closer to bedtime.

Tracking your added salt and sugar intake is easy, but it involves budgeting time for reading labels at the supermarket. Every packaged product is supposed to have nutrition information and a list of ingredients on the label or wrapping. Its chart of nutritional content will tell you how much sodium, sugar, fiber, and other components a food has *per serving*, so you need to look at how many servings are in the package. If the sodium content per serving in, say, a can of soup is 600 mg, but you consider lunch to be a full can of soup, then double the amount of added sodium, because soups are two servings per can.

It may sound daunting, but, like your food diary, checking content labels becomes second nature. There are also quick fixes to reduce added sodium and sugar from foods that can or will be cooked in water, such as discarding the liquid in the can and rinsing the product. That will give you lower numbers to enter in your records.

Another physiological phenomenon you can't exactly track but can try to help along is the gut-brain axis.[26]

There's a direct neural connection between the human digestive system and the brain called the vagus nerve. Its function is depressed by emotions such as stress and is enhanced by "good" bacteria in the gut, which help neurons in the gut produce neurotransmitters like serotonin, a chemical that contributes to a feeling of well-being. Good gut microbes also produce other chemicals that can affect brain function. Encouraging the production of good gut bacteria is the purpose of foods called probiotics.

Only testing can determine your level of good and bad gut bacteria, but you can track your intake of foods that enhance the gut-brain axis. Omega-3 fats, found in oily fish, and fermented foods, such as yogurt, kefir, and sauerkraut, have a positive effect on brain activity. High-fiber foods, such as whole grains, nuts, seeds, and many fruits and vegetables, can reduce the stress hormone cortisol. Tryptophan—found in turkey, eggs, and cheese—converts to serotonin. Foods rich in polyphenols, such as coffee, olive oil, green tea, and cocoa, may improve cognition. Remember, everything in moderation.

Another way to track health is through screening, which can be the first step in signaling fixable health problems. Women already are encouraged to perform breast self-exams once a month to feel for lumps that may be cancerous tumors, to have regular mammograms after age forty, and to visit a gynecologist regularly. Women also can have a Pap smear every year to detect cervical cancer.

Colon cancer, the most prevalent cancer worldwide, has a declining death rate because of advances in screening: the colonoscopy, which spots cancers and precancerous polyps, and products that allow people to take stool samples at home, send them in, and have them tested for traces of blood and cancerous DNA. For the upper gastrointestinal tract, there's endoscopy, which, like colonoscopy, uses a camera sent inside the body to take pictures and screen for problems in the esophagus and stomach.

Testing, even from mass-marketed companies such as 23andMe.com, can find genes that predispose people to certain illnesses. A good example is the test for the BRCA1 and BRCA2 genes, which are significant markers for future breast cancer. The PSA (prostate-specific antigen) test measures a protein that, in high enough evidence, can predict prostate cancer. The most detailed tests can spot whatever is out of balance in someone's body, catching malignancies early or heading them off altogether.

If you sign up for comprehensive screening such as that offered by Health Nucleus or Fountain Life, you can get a granular look at where you are healthwise and what you might be facing.

Where many cardiologists offer an angiogram evaluated by fluoroscopy, for example, these programs will take a three-dimensional CT scan of your heart enhanced by artificial intelligence. Dye is injected that will show calcified and noncalcified plaque buildup in the heart; the noncalcified is more dangerous because it can break off and move to block an artery, causing a heart attack. That's why from time to time you hear about an athlete who drops dead of a sudden heart attack; they didn't know they had plaque in their bodies that could move around and block an artery. Meanwhile, the AI algorithm can find information in the scan not visible to even the trained eye of the specialist.

Comprehensive programs also take a deep dive into blood work. Besides the usual lab tests doctors order—hemoglobin, A1c, cholesterol, liver and kidney enzymes, vitamin levels, and a host of others—the programs include the Galleri® Test, which can find markers in the blood for fifty different types of cancer. This test can detect cancer before it produces any symptoms, let alone spreads, reducing the severity of treatment and extending the proportion of people who live more than five years after diagnosis. Currently the medical establishment routinely screens for just five cancers: breast, cervical, prostate, lung, and colorectal. The Galleri® Test has a much wider range.

I can't overstate how important it is for people to take advantage of recent advances in screening and testing. For the cost of a family vacation, you can find out what health issues you have or may have and be able to push back the date of their effective onset. If you can take time for a week's holiday, you have the time set aside to monitor your health with the same care that you used to build up a success business and a secure portfolio. And that will likely afford you many more holidays and family vacations in the years to come.

In the final analysis, tracking your health is all about mindfulness. Many people still live out the maxims "Ignorance is bliss" and "What you don't know can't hurt you." They couldn't be more mistaken because only by *knowing* can you take responsibility for your own well-being. A sense of mindfulness about your health keeps it on the front burner and prevents you from forgetting that *you* have to take care of yourself. If instead you cultivate ignorance about your wellness, you take control out of your hands and place it in the hands of doctors, nurses, relatives, assisted-living attendants, and other third parties. Ignorance leads to dependency on people who know more than you do, while mindfulness encourages personal learning and independence.

Tracking your health, systematically and honestly, puts the numbers that measure your habits right in front of you. To be fair, it isn't always fun to review this information, especially when it indicates some needed dietary and exercise changes you may not like. But, fun or not, it can set you on the path to a longer and more active life. Would you rather have your cancer caught at stage 1, when there's a 95 percent survival rate after five years, or at stage 4, when the survival rate drops to 5 percent? Would you rather have a stent put in to expand an artery or drop dead on the tennis court because the artery became 100 percent blocked? Which is better: knowing and acting on high creatinine levels or waving away the numbers, only to wind up visiting a dialysis center three times a week because of kidney failure? Tracking is mindfulness by the numbers, and mindfulness is one of the qualities that will help you attain a long, healthy life.

CHAPTER 10

You Can't Be Well without Good Mental Health

All eyes in the stadium were on Tampa Bay wide receiver Antonio Brown when he melted down in East Rutherford, New Jersey, during a third-quarter offensive drive—and the eyes of the world were on him minutes later when footage of his behavior was put on the Internet and quickly went viral.[27]

Brown had been complaining about an injured ankle, but he had suited up for Tampa Bay's game against the New York Jets on January 2, 2022, and he had helped gain some yardage for the Buccaneers. He was on the sidelines, arguing with head coach Bruce Arians, when suddenly he broke away, stripped off his jersey and shoulder pads, then his undershirt. Brown then ran shirtless across the Jets' end zone while the teams were on the field, jumping and playing to the crowd until he disappeared into the locker room. He was cut from the team four days later.

It wasn't Brown's first spate of inappropriate behavior. He'd been convicted of reckless driving, sued for sexual assault, suspended from the NFL for attacking the driver of a moving van, and suspended again for faking a COVID-19 vaccination card. The Bucs kept him on the roster only because he was valuable to the team. The incident at MetLife Stadium, though, was certainly Brown's most bizarre stunt, and it ended his NFL career at age thirty-three.

Sports commentators and fans spent the next week speculating why Brown went off in such a spectacular manner. Was he unbalanced? Had he developed chronic traumatic encephalopathy (CTE), brain damage caused by repeated blows to the head? Did the Bucs ignore an obvious problem? Brown denied having any mental health issues, and an MRI confirmed damage to his ankle, but he did say, "I have stress; I have things I need to work on."[28]

Dr. Lisa Post, who worked as a team psychologist for the NFL for thirteen years, told Fox Sports that being an NFL player "is inherently stressful in terms of the frequently unrealistic expectations and unrelenting scrutiny of fans and even family members, the lack of job security, [and] the physical demands of an often very brief professional football career."[29] Daurice Fountain, a wide receiver for the Kansas City Chiefs, called mental illness "a real reality for a lot of us in this business." He added, "Let's figure out a way to give [Brown] the help he needs."[30]

The best-publicized stories about mental fatigue and the onset of mental illness tend to feature either bloodshed ("But he was such a nice, quiet boy," one mystified neighbor says) or celebrity. Gymnast Simone Biles stepped away from competition and tennis ace Naomi Osaka left the Women's Tennis Association (WTA) pro tour because the stress became too much for them to carry. Chef Anthony Bourdain committed suicide, leaving behind an eleven-year-old daughter, and only after his death did news outlets report years of depression and musings about how he would kill himself. Lurid stories about famous CEOs, athletes, and performers coming out as addicted or mentally damaged surface every month, with reactions ranging from "Lock them up" to "Poor thing, I hope they can get help."

And then there are the rest of us.

Antonio Brown arguably had the connections, money, and status to get whatever assistance he needed— yet his meltdown was almost as ignominious as that of any homeless person who starts yelling on a street corner. What chance do those of us have who lack access to the best psychotherapists and the money to pay their fees?

The blazing parade of celebrities headed to treatment usually fails to shed light on less-than-famous people who need help with mental health issues and don't get it. Part of that has to do with the invisibility of mental illness. If someone has a physical problem, you can usually see evidence of that problem, such as a limp, the quick self-massage of a shoulder, or a wince or grunt when rising from a chair. But unless a person throws a punch or starts disrobing in the conference room, odd speech and behavior usually can be explained away.

There are many reasons that people, famous or not, keep quiet about mental health issues. One is shame—nobody wants to admit they have what many people see not as an illness but as a weakness or failing. Another is privacy—people with mental issues don't want their status out there because it may reflect badly on them, especially in business. For people in the public eye, mental illness raises questions such as, "Will coaches, team owners, agents, and teammates trust me? Will I lose my competitive edge?" For the not-so-famous, the stakes possibly are higher: "Will people want to invest with me or in me? Will my boss blame my illness for problems unrelated to it? Will I lose my job? Will I be able to get health and life insurance (or have to pay more for it)?"

Mental illness also carries a big stigma—undeservedly because it's beyond anyone's control. Because it's often associated with bizarre behaviors and detachment from reality, mental illness causes people to have certain negative expectations of those who suffer from it. Even when someone seems to be completely "normal" because of medication and other interventions, simply knowing they are receiving mental health treatment changes how people see them. Friends, family members, and coworkers may be waiting apprehensively for them to demonstrate those issues by word or deed. The behavior of many untreated people with mental illness feeds this fear.

Illnesses such as depression and bipolar disorder can be as disabling as Crohn's disease or arthritis. The great Pittsburgh quarterback Terry Bradshaw, known to younger audiences as a sportscaster, suffered from major depression. He would experience anxiety attacks when he got home from games, bursting into tears for no apparent reason. He also had attention deficit disorder (ADD), which made learning plays difficult. Bradshaw's anguish reached a breaking point in 1999 when his third wife asked for a divorce. The anxiety and depression deepened, and he began to self-medicate by drinking heavily. "I wasn't sure if I was going to drink myself to death," Bradshaw told a reporter.[31] That's when he sought help by taking antidepressants and talk therapy. A few years later, he began to speak publicly about his illness, hoping other people would take his example as an inspiration.

"You know what, I'm not ashamed of who I am," Bradshaw said at a meeting of the American Psychiatric Association in 2010. "It's the way I was made. I just got some issues here, and I dealt with them. And I'm proud of it."[32]

Athletes, in fact, have been visible leaders in recent years in the effort to destigmatize mental illness. Olympic swimmer Michael Phelps said in 2018 that he suffered from ADD and depression and had thought about killing himself after the 2012 Games in London.[33] I've already mentioned Antonio Brown, Simone Biles, and Naomi Osaka. In 2021, the Irsay family, owners of the Indianapolis Colts, began a campaign called "Kicking the Stigma" to raise consciousness about mental health issues, which were present among the Irsays—and are present among professional football players.

"[We're] telling everybody that it is okay to not be okay," said Kalen Jackson, granddaughter of Irsay patriarch Bob Irsay and a Colts executive.[34]

Even when you focus on mental health as an issue for noncelebrities, you're still talking about people who carry the expectations of others. We financial planners tend to work with society's more affluent investors. Most people who come to us with the profits of a long-term career are good at what they do: hardworking, resourceful, and smart enough about money to have accumulated enough wealth to seek out an investing expert. What mental health problems could they possibly have?

The truth is, they, too, can carry a lot of weight on their shoulders—a different type of weight than the one carried by people who struggle to make ends meet, but it's weight all the same. Since the middle of the twentieth century, there has been an expectation that anyone with brains, education, and a modicum of natural talent who is willing to work hard can become successful. That puts a lot of pressure on kids who show, from an early age, that they're smart, attractive, and/or good at something—whether that something is academics, music, acting, sports, or any other established field. It even applies to children with talent for something less tangible, such as sociability or charm. This pressure has only grown from the time I was a child; I certainly wouldn't want to face the expectations that high-achieving teenagers withstand today.

As young adults, these kids go through college and graduate school and enter professional life, some hired straight from school by successful practices and companies, and some encountering obstacles along the way. As they become successful, the young adults take on responsibilities such as spouses, children, and home-ownership, which means they have to deal with the real world, not the sheltered environment they may have enjoyed previously.

By their late twenties and early thirties, when they really need to start thinking about putting money away for the future, many of these financially successful adults are facing challenges such as these:

- Work pressures such as promotion opportunities and performance expectations
- Cash outflow for mortgage, vehicles, tuition (both repayment and saving for kids' tuition), and lifestyle
- Problems with their marriage or other relationships
- Emotional factors involving their children, especially as the kids get older
- Residual issues with parents, especially as parents age
- Physical health concerns, including possible substance abuse
- Unresolved psychological issues, such as childhood abuse or PTSD

I've definitely seen some of these problems in my wealth management practice. Anxiety about money is common, even among people who are good wage-earners. Some folks come in worried about their children for one reason or another. There were times when I've smelled alcohol on people's breaths in my meetings—not often, but sometimes. I knew which clients had challenges—and I had to be extra careful about how to deal with their money because I knew they weren't opening up to me.

Even a few of these issues create hefty burdens. Yet, while acknowledging problems is the crucial first step, many believe *admitting* them can be seen as a show of weakness. A high-powered lawyer, surgeon, or C-suite aspirant is no more willing to admit to suffering from depression or anxiety than a professional athlete is to complain of a sore shoulder. He's ashamed to be seen as less than strong. She's sure any indication of vulnerability will be used against her.

So they don't get the help they need—neither the physical help nor the psychological help. They don't enjoy the money they earn when they're still young enough to enjoy it, and they won't be healthy enough to enjoy it after they retire.

Money can cushion some of the stress for celebrities, who can buy treatment and access to facilities that most of us can only dream of. And they can buy privacy—secrecy about rehab, plastic surgery, or visits to neurologists and orthopedists. If they do come out as troubled, well, hey, they're public figures; they're seen as courageous trendsetters. Their example may convince the average citizen that if it's OK for a superstar to get treated for depression, it's OK for them too. However, it can also work the other way. The average Joe might say, "That's fine for them, but I couldn't get away with it." Beliefs like that are what led me to be extra-encouraging to those who are brave enough to talk about their struggles. For example, when a new client recently told me he'd been diagnosed with depression, I congratulated him, because I thought he was really courageous to open up to me.

I'm sensitized to mental health issues because I grew up in the 1960s and 1970s with a disabled sister. My younger sister, Amy, was born with a genetic mutation—a complete fluke—that caused her to have severe developmental deficits. This was at a time when families with developmentally delayed children were still putting them in institutions because having a disabled child was not popular and was frankly embarrassing.

The need to provide for a disabled family member comes up in discussions about money more than you'd think. I ask clients how money played a part in their childhoods, and they bring up topics unrelated to money, such as PTSD, disability, and substance abuse. This often touches on money—after all, a dad who drinks to excess is unlikely to be a dad who handles money well—but the money issue is often tangential. I've had successful female clients who told me about growing up in rough households and having to fend for themselves at an early age. They realized the adults in their lives were not going to teach them what they needed to know, so they became resourceful and learned by themselves how to make money and save it. I can understand people who faced challenges while they were growing up because I did too.

Mental health issues can wreak havoc with trust. I got a call recently from a client who believed he was experiencing the early stages of dementia. My response was to invite the client to my office with everyone who might have a stake in his financial affairs, especially his wife and kids, possibly a trusted friend, because the first thing you have to do is establish who has permission to know about the client's financial dealings and, more important, who has control over the client's finances.

The husband may be afraid that if his wife or one of his children has power of attorney, that person will take all the money. The family may be afraid that if Dad keeps control, he'll spend all the money on extravagant items or bad investments. It's my job to talk them all down and let them know that nothing nefarious is going to happen. No one is going to run off with Dad's money. Dad is always going to know where his money is and what's being done with it. That usually calms down Mom and Dad.

But it may not calm down the adult children. This is another area that involves trust. I try to get all the children involved, often because they can be more objective and less emotional than the parents when it comes to how the parents' money should be spent. But that isn't always the case. Sometimes the one who gets the power of attorney and becomes the arbiter of the funds, no matter how qualified that child is, becomes the object of resentment by the other kids. Maybe the eldest child objects if he isn't the one designated; maybe the child who's an executive and a control freak wants to be in the driver's seat. At the end of the day, the child who knows the parents' finances best and has the best head for money should be in charge.

If the argument gets bad enough, I don't hesitate to advise a family to find a therapist. I'll tell them that I'm no expert, but I grew up in a family that was helped by therapy, and I know how much it can help iron out issues. I even offer to find the therapist for them.

It's a lot for a financial planner to deal with. Lines of communication have become much more complicated since I started in this business. These days, my staff members have to be hyperaware of who gets informed about what so they don't give sensitive information to the wrong person. Thirty years ago, anyone could call our office and say she's the daughter of a client, and someone in the office would have probably talked to her and told her what she wanted to know. Today, financial planners have to have a list of trusted contacts—adult children, spouse, attorney, maybe accountant—and understand exactly what each person is entitled to know. The client may want one child, the one with power of attorney, to know more than the other sons and daughters.

There are other aspects of listening to personal and family problems, let alone giving advice about them, that a financial planner has to consider seriously. One is the need to be absolutely genuine about wanting to hear about psychological details because otherwise the advisor isn't really trying to help the clients and, in fact, *can't* help them. It doesn't make sense to ask a client about sensitive psychological issues and then say, "Oh, that's a shame, good luck with that."

Financial advisors who counsel on mental health issues also have to make it clear that they are *not* trained as doctors or psychotherapists, and it's important for clients to seek professional help for important issues that come up. "I will give you my perspective," I tell clients, "but mine is only one viewpoint, and it isn't that of a psychologist." I could be the outlier if five therapists say they believe my view is way off base. I play down my role as an advisor on anything other than money because the problem itself is more important than how seriously a client takes me.

I want to help my clients as best I can, and if that means listening and then keeping my mouth shut, with advice or anything else, that's fine. Sometimes all clients want is a shoulder to cry on, a place to be heard, so I have no problem with clients unloading on me, then finding their own way through their problems. If the client really wants advice—a possible solution, a first step—I can handle that too. What's important is that I clarify what the client wants, and that's best accomplished simply by asking, "You've given me this information. What do you want me to do with it?" The response from the client may be one of the following:

- Do nothing.
- Please recommend the first step toward a resolution of my problem.
- Please recommend a plan of action.
- Let me get back to you on that.

I always clarify my role by telling them that because I'm not a mental health professional, I may not be the only practitioner they should consult on a topic that isn't only about money.

It's a delicate balance. If I'm making a client $100,000, $500,000, or $1 million a year in appreciation and interest, and if that client is still waking up every morning depressed or anxious about his life, what is my responsibility? Strictly speaking, it is only to keep expanding his financial wealth. But if listening to their troubles and suggesting a first step toward being *less* depressed or anxious is within my capability, why wouldn't—why *shouldn't*—I do that? It's an expression of my regard for the client that I want to help, and the first step I suggest is usually a trip to a qualified therapist.

The fact is, financial planners have acted as unofficial advisors on nonmoney issues for years. I once helped one of my top clients enter a rehab program. He was a very intelligent man, a CEO type, but I had to arrange an intervention on the phone with his family. They trusted me because I told them I wasn't a licensed therapist, but I'd been through an intervention with a family friend who was a drinker. I told them, "If you'd like me to put together an intervention and then give you some guidance on what the next steps might be, I can do that." They allowed me to make some calls and help find a specialist who did interventions. Fortunately, that situation worked out. There's a lot to be said for "been there, done that."

A financial advisor really is positioned to talk about mental health issues with clients because the advisor already knows a lot about the client. Sometimes the advisor has knowledge the spouse and the rest of the family don't have. The financial advisor also tends to be in touch with the client a lot more than other professionals are. We're required to communicate with clients at least once a year, and most of us check in much more frequently. An attorney helps people with personal matters, too, but the attorney generally is seen on an "as needed" basis, for example, to draft, change, or facilitate the execution of a will. I have clients who haven't talked with their lawyers in years because nothing has come up that requires one.

The accountant who calculates someone's taxes every year also isn't the right person with whom to discuss emotional issues, not so much because they're all about numbers but because they're focused on limited time frames. The accountant's focus is on the past year: How much income did you have? What were its sources? Did you do anything that would cause you to pay less in taxes than you did last year? How much do you owe? And her thinking about the future generally covers just the coming year: Do you expect your income to change this year? Can you do anything during the current year to create a lower tax liability this time next year?

Wealth managers are more suited to help people with personal matters because money really touches everything in people's lives, and they think long-term— twenty, thirty, forty years ahead. Is it time to take out life insurance? What about long-term care? How do we set up a college fund for our newborn child? How should we provide for our special needs child after we're gone? And the biggest question: How much do we need to put away to increase the odds of a comfortable retirement? If the advisor is in touch with all the different aspects of a client's life because they involve money, he's probably going to hear the stories behind the decisions the client needs to make.

For example, we hear why clients change the beneficiaries on their IRAs, why the client wants to dissolve a trust fund or stop an allowance, why one client thinks she'll live well past the average life span, and what makes another think he'll never have grandchildren. We may suspect dementia or a lapse in judgment if a client suddenly wants to spend $100,000 on a necklace—and we can advise against the purchase, notify compliance, and let them have the necessary follow-up discussions to make sure we're doing our due diligence in protecting a client's wealth from their own potential health problems.

Financial advisors are uniquely positioned to probe and give feedback because the daily decisions we make and the daily topics we deal with are so intertwined with life that it's surprising we don't get formal training on health and wellness. A certified financial planner has a fiduciary obligation to clients; in other words, we're required to make decisions that are in the best interests of the client, and if we don't know what those interests are, if we don't ask the questions that allow us to know the client well, we can be held liable for allowing them to make bad decisions.

Mental health, then, is an important component in the work we do. We need to introduce scorecards for our clients not just about money and not just about physical health but about mental issues. The more we know about our clients' minds and emotions, the better equipped we are to help them make good decisions for the long term and to advise them on those decisions. We want our clients to understand what Simone Biles learned while still a teenager: that mental health comes first if you want to succeed at *and* enjoy what you're doing with your life.

CHAPTER 11

Living Long, Living Rich

have a client who has about $750,000 invested with me. I've known this guy forever—he worked as a salesman thirty-five years ago, and he's been a client for twenty years. Recently we had a review of his portfolio, and he was very pleased; his holdings had gone up 75 percent over the past five years. But he told me something sad: "My only regret is that my wife isn't healthy enough for us to enjoy the money." She wasn't at death's door, thank goodness, but she wasn't well. Basically, he was saying to me, "You've done everything right as my planner, and I'm not upset with *you*. I just wish my wife were healthier so we could enjoy the money together."

Warren Buffett was well aware of that dilemma when, in 2019, he offered an audience of Millennials a wise nugget of advice about wealth, health, and priorities:

Imagine that you had a car and that was the only car you'd have for your entire lifetime. Of course, you'd care for it well, changing the oil more frequently than necessary, driving carefully, et cetera. Now, consider that you only have one mind and one body. Prepare them for life, care for them. You can enhance your mind over time. A person's main asset is themselves, so preserve and enhance yourself.[35]

The concept of living rich while living long always reminds me of the life of actress and screenwriter Ruth Gordon, known to audiences of a certain age for the movies *Rosemary's Baby* and *Harold and Maude*. Gordon lived to be almost eighty-nine. She worked as an actress pretty much until her death in 1985, and she was working on a new play the morning before she succumbed to a massive stroke with her husband at her side. Wouldn't it be wonderful if every death occurred that way—suddenly, peacefully, and at an active, advanced age?[36]

Gordon's later life seems to be the exception, though. If you're in your early eighties, you've already beaten your life expectancy at birth by about a decade; a child born in the United States in 1940 was expected to live to about seventy, which may be why today we think of a long life to mean living past eighty. However, for most of us, the last four or five years of that long life, maybe more, are spent with illness, debility, depression, and pain, subject to so many ways to feel bad that they rarely seem worth enduring. That's why *Lifespan* author David Sinclair sees aging as the disease, not the maladies that accompany it.

Those last years should be reflective, instructive, even productive. Older people should be able not only to witness their grandchildren's weddings but to dance at them. They should enjoy poker nights, trade their walkers for long walks, write their memoirs or research, and write the book they've been thinking about for twenty years. Instead, they (and often their middle-aged children) are caught up in rising healthcare costs for the problems Sinclair sees as symptoms of aging, such as heart disease, cancer, kidney and liver failure, effects of diabetes, and neurodegenerative disease. Their days are filled with doctors' appointments and reminders to take pills rather than visits to museums and lunches with friends. Their final weeks are spent in hospital beds, hooked up to monitors and IV bags, not cruising toward a sunset in an RV.

That isn't the vision we want for our clients in Balanced Wealth. If people can potentially have an extra ten or fifteen years of life,[37] we want those years to be happy and healthy because those are years to watch your grandchildren grow up, graduate from school, get married, have kids of their own. And after you've put in a lifetime of hard work into building your retirement fund, and your financial advisor has worked hard to keep it safe and make it grow, we want you to maintain the same quality of life you've enjoyed during your working years.

You may have heard people say, "Being a grandparent is so much fun that I wish I could have done that first!" To have that fun, you need enough energy and positivity to take grandchildren to ball games and the movies, answer a million questions, relate your history, go hiking, and take road trips. Some people wish they could take the wisdom and self-awareness they have at seventy back to the years when they were raising their children. Without fear of dependency, people can use those extra ten or fifteen years for imparting wisdom and helping their kids and grandkids head off mistakes—or for mending damaged relationships.

People who live long, productive lives tend to have a *purpose*, a set of goals or reasons for living past retirement age. Otherwise, they face the "three Ds" that are said to be the fate for people who retire without a plan: divorce, depression, and death. Dan Sullivan, founder of Strategic Coach, points out that people who have a purpose in life almost always live longer.[38] That purpose may be related to charitable work, lifelong learning, travel, a personal project, or anything other than three rounds of golf a week (as enticing as that might sound).

If you want proof, let's go back to the earliest days of the American republic. According to the National

Institutes of Health, the life expectancy for white males at birth in the United States from 1790 to 1840 was between thirty-nine and forty-four years, although a boy who survived to age twenty had an expectation of making it closer to age sixty.[39] That's probably why the drafters of the US Constitution chose thirty-five as the minimum age for a US president; they wanted presidents to be seasoned veterans of life who could nonetheless survive more than one term.

Look at the ages attained by almost all the Founding Fathers:

Name	Dates	Age at Death	Contributions to US History
Benjamin Franklin	1706–1790	84	Assisted in drafting Declaration of Independence and Constitution; diplomat to France
Samuel Adams	1722–1803	81	Powerful influencer in bringing colonies to revolt against Britain
George Washington	1732–1799	67	First US president (1789–1797) after victory as general in American Revolution
John Adams	1735–1826	90	Assisted in drafting Declaration of Independence; second US president (1797–1801)

Name	Dates	Age at Death	Contributions to US History
Thomas Jefferson	1743–1826	83	Primary writer, Declaration of Independence; third US president (1801–1809)
John Jay	1745–1829	83	Served First and Second Continental Congresses; first chief justice of the US Supreme Court
James Madison	1751–1836	85	Primary writer, US Constitution and Bill of Rights; fourth US president (1809–1817)
Alexander Hamilton	1755–1804	49	Leader in effort to ratify Constitution; first US secretary of the Treasury
Aaron Burr	1756–1836	80	Senator; third US vice president; helped form early political party
James Monroe	1758–1831	83	Delegate to Continental Congress; Sec. of State; fifth US president (1817–1825)

For some of these men, their most productive years as statesmen came late in life, and several held public office for years after their participation as Founders. Even those whose later lives were spent away from public service mostly remained active as writers and political philosophers. The outlier in the group, Alexander Hamilton, died young not because of disease but because Aaron Burr shot him in a duel. For his part, Burr, whose political career ended when he killed Hamilton, stayed busy for thirty years with travel and financial deals.

This isn't just ancient political history. Our forty-fifth and forty-sixth US presidents were elected in their seventies, and Congress is replete with members in their seventies and eighties. Wherever they fall on the political spectrum, they continue to serve from a sense of purpose. And that's only one field. Consider the thousands of scientists, academics, artists, and professionals who ply their crafts into old age or find another channel—teaching, coaching, advocacy—in which to remain active. Having purpose in life keeps them young, and it can do the same for you.

Crucial to many folks' efforts to live a healthy retirement is keeping the mind active, especially by learning something new. There are so many ways to do that! Road Scholar offers hundreds of experiences around the world (and many at home, virtually). Participants can study fields as diverse as wildlife in Costa Rica and artwork in Italy. The trips last about as long as a typical cruise and are a lot more stimulating. Community colleges offer courses on almost every subject imaginable, and local recreation centers are good places to find classes on aspects of computer technology. Remember, too, that it is never too late to start learning a new language.

SCORE, a national organization associated with the Small Business Administration, has 250 local offices matching small business owners with successful entrepreneurs who volunteer as mentors to provide advice and support. Experience Corps, a partner in the AARP Foundation, places people fifty and older with children in grades K–3 who are struggling to learn how to read. These are only two of the many ways individuals can help their communities using methods that both protect and expand people's wisdom.

Think of how many people a retiree could help during those extra ten or fifteen years of vigorous life. They're in a perfect place in their lives to help people who need it if they have time, money, and good physical health. A seventy-year-old with vitality and mobility can help build houses for an organization such as Habitat for Humanity or volunteer for a charitable food pantry. Later, when the body weakens but the mind is still sharp, that same retiree, at eighty-something, can become a tutor or mentor for a youngster.

That's a great role for an older adult. Sometimes kids don't have support at home and need someone to talk to. They might be able to open up to someone older, someone who has outlived the judgmental attitudes they had when younger, someone who's no longer fighting the parent-child battles. At the same time, the older adult has experience and, possibly, a longer and wider view of the world than the young person does. Working with children allows people with wisdom, knowledge, and experience to pass those gifts to many more members of a younger generation than just their own grandchildren.

Imagine a cadre of adults who take advantage of the progress in medical technology and arrive at age ninety with abilities far beyond what their own parents had at sixty-five. There could be thousands of them, serving as wonderful role models to later generations. Think of all their grandchildren marveling at how vigorous and sharp Grandma and Pops are compared to most older people they know. They determine to do what their grandparents did to maintain their health into old age, and there you have it: a generational transfer of not just wealth but health.

What does it mean to live rich? It means being able to learn new things and have new experiences when most of your contemporaries are either too feeble to leave the house or get into trouble when they do. It means being able to donate to hospitals and foundations that support scientists who are looking for the cure for diseases that have frightened people for decades, even centuries, or support geneticists who are trying to find a way to sequence the human genome more effectively but less expensively. It means handing down a lifestyle of good health, activity, and mental acuity from one generation to another and being able to help the people you love to live that lifestyle.

It amazes me how often people of significant means are reluctant to spend money on their health. One of my clients who has millions of dollars invested with me says he's thinking of going to a longevity center in New Jersey to get a comprehensive checkup. This longevity service is similar to Health Nucleus and Fountain Life in that you get thorough screening for many diseases, but it charges more in the $3,000 to $5,000 range because it doesn't provide advanced services such as genome sequencing. This client could find the $15,000 for a more complete workup under his sofa cushions, but he's just *thinking* of going to the New Jersey center.

Some of my clients are doing well but still think of themselves as unable to afford a subscription to a place such as Health Nucleus. Let me give you a hypothetical example that can put this investment in your health into perspective. If I'm managing a portfolio worth $3 million, $15,000 represents 0.5 percent of the client's holdings, which is negligible. Even if the client considers the cost of Health Nucleus against income, $15,000 might represent only a few weeks' interest on a diversified portfolio of $3 million. Or suppose the client has holdings of $1 million and her yearly income with Social Security and such is $70,000, but they're very frugal and live on $50,000 a year—$20,000 less than their Social Security income. Wouldn't $15,000 of that extra $20,000 be money well spent? Even if the cost of a Health Nucleus subscription was a stretch, it's still worth giving up one vacation to take steps toward ten to fifteen more good years.

Looking after your health is a matter of priorities more than money. If you're working with a financial planner, you should at least have enough money saved to afford high-end healthcare in addition to a primary care physician and specialists. This should be a psychological choice, not a financial one. You have to love yourself enough and have enough self-worth to decide that your health and well-being are important enough to spend serious money on. It's the best investment you will ever make.

Most people who sign up for high-end medical screenings don't have to see it as an either-or proposition. I'm trying, with *The Balanced Wealth Approach*, to encourage folks to be "both/and" people, to operate in a way that lets them meet their goals without sacrificing other pursuits. Both/and people live rich. They buy the Tesla and take the trip around the world. They pay their kids' ways through graduate school and still buy the vacation house. They treat themselves to the best healthcare available and give money to charity.

The alternative is the either-or life, in which people think they have to choose between two good things. Eventually, the need for good healthcare will make them think they have to choose between healthy longevity and a lifestyle that maintains some luxury. They don't have to be either-or about that. They don't have to risk dying of something stupid to finance a cruise. They can look after their health, then take the cruise, and come home to the good news that they're fine, or a tumor was caught at stage zero, or a few changes in diet and exercise can reverse their type 2 diabetes.

It is generally accepted in the financial services industry that a 60 percent stock and 40 percent bond allocation is considered a balanced portfolio. The stocks are subject to volatility, but over time, they tend to grow in value or can be replaced by stronger ones. The bonds are designed to provide stability and pay periodic interest dividends. Investors who want the sizable earnings of successful stocks throughout their portfolios may put all their money into stocks, but if they do, they're in for a white-knuckle financial ride.

You've probably been on an airplane when the weather became turbulent and caused the plane to shake or even dive. You know intellectually that the pilot is trained to fly through the turbulence without real danger, but you're still terrified the plane may crash or break up. Most flyers don't want a white-knuckle trip.

Suppose the pilot flying you from Boston to Chicago gave you two choices:

1) There's a storm brewing west of Boston; if you feel a lot of turbulence, that's the reason, but I'll get you to Chicago safely and on time.

2) I can reroute the plane south, toward Atlanta, but you'll get to Chicago at least an hour late. The investors

who fancy themselves risk-takers might say, "Sure, fly through the storm," but halfway through the turbulence they turn into George Jetson yelling, "Jane, get me off this crazy thing!"

Just as most folks want balance in their portfolios, they want balance in their lives. I wish I had a dollar for every newspaper, magazine, and online article published since the introduction of the smartphone that discusses work-life balance. It's always been difficult to find the off switch for work, to be fully present for every movie, soccer game, and family dinner. But developments such as the smartphone and Zoom have wired us even more firmly to our jobs, making us accessible 24/7/365. That's a problem because part of living rich is having that off switch, being able to detach from the quotidian and enjoy the moment.

When the COVID-19 pandemic hit and we all started working from home, it looked for a minute as if we were getting our lives back; we could wear sweats while we worked, we could put in a load of laundry, work out, or even take a walk outside whenever we wanted. But once management figured out that it could keep us tethered with technology, we lost a lot of that freedom.

When meetings were in person, life could get in the way. You might miss a meeting because traffic was terrible, or your kid missed her bus and you had to take her to school. Then the pandemic trapped us in our homes, there was no traffic, and your kid wasn't going to school.

Life became one Zoom meeting after another, and you had to be there unless your Wi-Fi failed. Now, Zoom burnout is a real thing, and it isn't going to let up because so many people are going to continue working remotely for the foreseeable future. Some don't want to come back to the office because working from home is simply more convenient. Others are anxious about returning because of health concerns; they don't want to be exposed to pathogens or to bring them home.

The pandemic, by the way, wreaked havoc with the healthcare system. Doctors and nurses working in hospitals were stretched beyond their limits—no work-life balance for them. It was a terrible time to get sick with anything, because acute COVID cases pushed others to the back of the line. Suddenly cancer surgery was deemed elective; it didn't matter if your tumor was detected early because you had to wait to have it removed, worrying all the time that it was getting bigger and spreading. And overworked personnel made many more medical mistakes than they did before the pandemic. Doctors with practices outside hospitals felt the stress of empty waiting rooms and falling revenues.

We're still feeling the effects of the "Great Resignation" of 2021, when a wave of employees left jobs, some permanently. They may have more balance in their lives, but they left many small-business owners and links in the supply chain in the lurch, causing the work they had done to fall on the backs of restaurant owners and shopkeepers who found themselves understaffed. This, too, is happening in the healthcare field, where personnel are leaving for more lucrative work.

Stephen Covey was right: "The challenge of work-life balance is without question one of the most significant struggles faced by modern man."[40] I meet so many people who are burning out because when you have your phone turned on, your office is in your pocket. Your partners and associates could probably get to you in Machu Picchu, and even if they don't, you could still keep cleaning out your inbox, keeping up with what's happening in the office, letting people know that you are available *"as a last resort."* Then there are the people whose jobs require them to sleep with their mobile phones. These are all people who either must be in close touch with their work at all times or at least feel as if they must. But living rich is more than being tops at your work. How do you convince workaholics they can flip the off switch and take time to enjoy life away from work?

Part of the persuasion involves paying attention to your health scorecard because if you monitor your diet and sleep, seek out opportunities for exercise, and take steps to reduce the stress in your life, *by definition* you're taking time away from the daily pressures of work. Being more mindful of what you eat takes more time than grabbing fast food. An hour in a yoga class is an hour away from the office and so is getting the additional hour of sleep you need. Even five minutes of controlled deep breathing represents five minutes of taking time for your own needs. You may not be able to change the boss you're working for (especially if you're the boss), but you can take steps away from work that might have a big impact on your life.

I tend to alternate between health mindfulness and work concerns. I start almost every day with meditation—but then I pick up my phone and see what appointments I have during the day. After that, though, I go straight to my Ōura Ring® and check my sleep number and my readiness score, which tell me my body temperature, respiratory rate, and how my heart rate varied during the night. For that moment, I channel my addiction to numbers and measurement into something that's about my health and well-being rather than checking text messages and emails. It's a small thing, but it tells you something about my priorities.

Here's the real balancing act: being able to reschedule meetings and appointments so that you can take care of your health at the same time you handle your workload. If you need an hour at the gym or a visit to the sauna, there are ways to make that happen if you have a schedule with some flexibility. If you're fortunate enough to get to a point where you've made enough money to provide for your future—but you are years from wanting to quit working—you can start planning your work around your well-being and stop snatching fleeting moments of self-care.

Let's say you get to karate on a Monday night, but Tuesday is a long day of back-to-back meetings, and you can't get the exercise you want. If you're dragging the next morning, it's time to move a couple of appointments around and get to the gym or book a massage. If you're in a position of authority, you can tell your team not to overstuff your schedule, and every once in a while, when the stars align, especially after a couple of really hectic workdays, you can take a day off.

Dan Sullivan of Strategic Coach describes a day away from work as a Free Day™, when you do no work-related activities. He also distinguishes what he calls Buffer Days™ from regular workdays. These are days you use to realign, refocus priorities, examine what you're working on, and identify what needs your attention. That's another part of the work-life balancing act.

In fact, Sullivan advises entrepreneurs to take a cue from some of the most financially successful people in our society: professional athletes and star entertainers. They work hard when they work, but a relatively small number of their hours are spent performing in public—playing in a game, acting on a sound stage, performing in a concert. Sullivan considers days spent training, practicing, or rehearsing to be Buffer Days, as opposed to Free Days when they shut everything down and relax. He advises business leaders to emulate these top earners: Take a look at your calendar for the next quarter; decide which days are going to be Free Days and which will be Buffer Days. For entrepreneurs, those might be days for strategic planning and revisioning. The rest are workdays or Focus Days™—time for doing the activities you do best and that generate income for your business. Sullivan insists that people who follow this strategy will make more money than the people who spend eighty hours a week in the office.

Suppose you were told you could work only three days next week. You'd have to prioritize. You'd have to decide who the people are whom you really have to see: the clients most important to your operation, the colleagues who enhance your capabilities, the client who writes you the largest check. That's what Dan Sullivan advises.

Also, you can improve your work-life balance by focusing on what you do best and gives you the most energy, and delegate the rest. If your strength is seeing the big picture and being able to explain that vision to clients, but you aren't as able to break down the numbers and explain exactly how your vision is doable, you need to delegate that part of the process to someone who revels in the details. A movie producer hires a stunt man because the actor's strength is acting, not falling out of a car. Remember the TV series *House, M.D.*? Dr. House was a star diagnostician who trained other doctors to become excellent diagnosticians. Because House had the personality of a buzz saw, he rarely spent time with the patients he diagnosed; he left direct patient care to members of his team, who were better prepared to work with people. If you focus on what you do best and delegate the rest, Dan Sullivan counsels, you'll have more time to spend on yourself.

Too many people beat themselves up for having a life outside the office. If I get stuff done at work before 5:00 p.m. and then go to a 6:00 p.m. class at the dojo, that's a great day. I don't berate myself because I didn't close a deal or make a million dollars. And I don't feel guilty because I think of the time at the dojo as the best part of the day. Where is it written that work has to make you as happy as the activities you do for fun or to take care of yourself?

It's important that *something* makes you happy if you want to live a long life. In *The Gap and The Gain,* Dan Sullivan mentions a longitudinal study of nuns who were asked, starting when they were young women, to keep journals. After many years, the researchers found that nuns who expressed positive thoughts in their journals lived an average of ten years longer than those whose entries were negative or neutral. At age eighty-five, 90 percent of the "contented" group of nuns were still alive, compared to 34 percent of nuns in the least happy group.

Other studies have shown that unhappy employees take fifteen more sick days a year than happy employees do and that people assessed with high happiness levels were able to fight off infection better than less happy subjects. Research such as this shows that a positive outlook on life lessens the impact of illness and stress on the body.[41]

Balancing work and life are also easier if you keep your debt to a minimum and your lifestyle on a sensible scale. Of course, everyone has to borrow money sometimes, to buy a house or car, put kids through school, buy a business, pay bills, and so on. But having a huge balloon payment over your head or staring down the barrel of years of high payments is really stressful. I've noticed over the years that my happiest and most relaxed clients were usually the ones who didn't borrow a lot of money and didn't carry any debt.

You don't have to live like a nun to keep debts from mounting; it's more a matter of spending on what's necessary for your comfort rather than on what will impress other people. I was never more stressed out than I was twenty years ago, when I had to borrow money to pay large legal bills. Keeping your spending in check and being more or less free of debt means you aren't making stressful decisions about money all the time—and it means that if a costly emergency does come up, you're in a better position to handle it than you would be if you were already carrying debt.

Under the heading of "Looking out for yourself," here is another bit of lifestyle advice: never be afraid to go to your doctor. Some people think a visit to a doctor is a sign of weakness. Others don't go because they don't want to hear bad news. Some know there's a reason they might get bad news, such as a familial tendency toward heart disease. Others fear that something is wrong with them, especially if something in their body hurts. ("I've been having headaches—I might have a brain tumor!") But some people are afraid even if they feel fine.

I was discussing the concept of comprehensive testing with one of my top clients, and he said, "Well, there are certain tests I wouldn't want them to run because what if they find out something?" He was specifically concerned about the likelihood that he would develop Alzheimer's disease because members of his family had developed it. If screening tests showed he was likely to develop Alzheimer's, too, he didn't want to know. "That's fine," I said, "that's your choice to make, but what if knowing now that you may develop dementia helps you ward it off?"

The head of Fountain Life told me that when he came up with the idea of in-depth screening for many different disorders, colleagues said to him, "What if you find out something's wrong?" Even *doctors* were worried about it! Rather than looking ahead to a world in which more and more medical problems can be solved, some doctors, of all people, are frightened that their patients might find out that they're facing a bump in the road.

People also fear getting a false positive as a test result or being told you have a certain disease when in fact you don't. The dread that someone feels hearing he's tested positive for an illness—from highly curable to life-threatening—can be profound, so much so that hearing he doesn't actually have the problem produces anger as much as it does relief. He might argue, "I'm just fine. If I hadn't gone to the doctor, I wouldn't have had this scare."

That's an understandable reaction to a mistake that can cause fear and disruption. People may start to tie up their worldly affairs, only to be told that they have to make a U-turn and put things back the way they were. Platitudes such as "You've been given a second chance!" or "These false positives are helpful teaching moments" don't make people feel much calmer.

While such a reaction to a false positive may be understandable, and a reluctance to see a doctor because you may get news you don't want to hear is understandable, neither is based on common sense. You have to set aside the fear that you are going to find out something you don't like, because otherwise, in five years you are going to find out something you *really* don't like.

The good work that doctors do greatly outweighs their errors. There's no benefit to medical science or to us in staying away from health professionals. They apply years of training and long hours in the field to taking care of us. We have enough talented physicians and researchers that many medical breakthroughs may be just around the corner, poised to join the advances that already let us catch medical problems early. Being afraid to consult people of expertise just doesn't make sense.

You don't want to hear:	You *really* don't want to hear:
"It's time to give up the nachos and burgers."	"Three of your arteries are 95 percent occluded by plaque. You need bypass surgery—right now."
"Your blood glucose is high, and it won't come down unless you eat fewer carbs and get some exercise."	"I'm afraid we're going to have to take your left foot now, and I'm not sure you can keep the other."
"You have a stage 1 malignancy at the bottom of one of your lungs, which we can remove cleanly."	"You have stage 4 lung cancer that has spread into your lymph nodes and spine."

Life is filled with difficult choices, and that includes choices about your health that range from nuisances to life-and-death scenarios. If living a long life means cutting out the foods I love, is that life worth living? If I develop dementia, who's the best person to look after me and my interests? If I carry the BRCA-1 gene that predicts breast cancer, do I want to know? Do I have to tell my daughters and cause them worry? Do I want a preventative double mastectomy?

Again, the key is whether you love yourself enough to hear the news you don't want to hear and to act on it: to wear the wearables, visit the doctor, feel hungry, let your muscles ache from the unaccustomed use, walk out of the room and breathe when the stress gets to be too much. Jon Kabat-Zinn, the former professor of medicine and mindfulness guru, says, "We take care of the future best by taking care of the present now."[42] In physical terms, that suggests how important it is to be conscious of what your body is telling you now, because whatever is already there is going to be there whether you know about it or not.

We want to win, but winning cannot happen without awareness, even if awareness is painful. We want to live long, but living long may involve sacrificing what you think you can't live without. We want to live richly, but we need to dispel the mindset that living richly is the same as living ostentatiously. The person who prevails in life is the person who accepts unwelcome news, assimilates the information that comes with that news, and takes action to turn that news of loss into gain.

CHAPTER 12

Let's Continue the Conversation

Congratulations! You have begun the journey toward Balanced Wealth. We've spent quite a bit of time together, talking about the importance of wellness, of balance, of staying on top of current trends. But with your enriched knowledge comes responsibility. The wellness and balance will come from your own efforts; you're the CEO of your health.

You can't point the finger at the doctor, your spouse, your mother, or your siblings. They can support you, but you're the one who has to change behavior. You can marvel at wearable tracking devices, precision health-care programs, and cutting-edge technologies, but they alone won't bring about the results you want. Only you can do that. You are charged with keeping a disciplined

THE BALANCED WEALTH APPROACH

approach to your health and wellness for the rest of your life, which I hope will now last decades longer.

No routine is perfect. You're human, and life gets in the way. The holidays. The out-of-town trips. The deadline to complete the project. Your second honeymoon. Your daughter's wedding. ("I paid for that food, and by God, I'm eating it!") One day you'll wake up and realize that you haven't monitored your blood pressure for two months, or you wear your Ōura Ring® faithfully but never check the readouts. You use your hectic schedule as an excuse for not working out—and for getting dinner from the vending machine. I've practiced martial arts week in, week out for more than forty years, but I've gotten busy and messed up. But I always get back in the dojo and say to myself, *I'm not giving up.* It's like they used to say at Weight Watchers: *lapse* is not the same as *collapse.*

One important thing for you to do is to build a wellness support system. Starting with your primary care physician, find practitioners you like, people you don't dread seeing. A chiropractor who has been vetted by an orthopedic surgeon really is a must because they can work wonders when you're stiff or hurting, and they have a good background in human anatomy. If you don't have a massage therapist, find one you like; I've come away from sessions feeling like a new person. You may need someone to advise you about inflammation, which is a looming, disorder-causing problem. Find people who will help you plan your diet, exercise routine, and sleep schedule. If you're reading this in your twenties or thirties, it isn't too early to pull together a support system; if you're in your fifties or sixties, it isn't too late.

No one can go it alone. You aren't a hermit subsisting on nuts and blades of grass in a mountain cave. You live around supermarkets and strip malls. You have a job, a family, a 401(k). You live around people, and some of those people were put on earth to be your allies in the struggle to be well and live a long, rich life. They are there to be part of your support system, to help you up when you fall, and to help you focus on the goal of being younger than you are.

I got where I am today as a financial advisor in part because of coaching programs such as Dan Sullivan's Strategic Coach and the coaching operation of Ron Carson, one of America's most prominent wealth managers. People in my target market might ask me something like, "You seem to have it all together. Why attend coaching programs?" I tell them that when I go to such a program, I learn from the best and the brightest and can share what I learn with my clients. They also break up my routine and help me recharge.

The coaching process is similar with health concerns. Especially if you subscribe to a precision healthcare program, you might wind up with a battalion of coaches, and you may even go out of town to get the care and advice you want. By establishing Balanced Wealth,

I'm asking to become part of your healthcare team as well as your financial team.

Why me? Well . . . why not? Over the years, I've learned so much about health, wellness, and longevity that I want to share it with others, starting with the people closest to me. I hope to attract people who perhaps have had a health scare or are looking at a future of debilitating illness and who say, "You know, this Tom guy not only knows what he's talking about, but he speaks my language. My old financial planner was so focused on the money that she never got to know me as a person. She didn't care if I lived or died, as long as I had money to pass along and documents that outlined where it went. Clearly, the human factor is in Tom's wheelhouse."

What do clients get from me in the Balanced Wealth program? I offer them the prospect—not the certainty, but the possibility—of ten or fifteen more good years of life. A life that's long and healthy enough that they can scratch items off their bucket lists and really enjoy them. A life in which clients don't regret having worked so hard, because they also took the time to be with the people they love and to pursue noncareer activities.

Basically, I hope Balanced Wealth creates a cohort of people who *don't* say,

- I wish I had stayed in touch with my friends.
- I wish I had a stronger relationship with my spouse, kids, grandkids, and siblings.

- I wish I had tried to write that novel/movie/memoir.
- I wish I had the time to learn something new.
- I wish we'd made that trip.
- I wish I'd had the time to give something back to society.

With ten or more good years after retirement, people can do those things: establish better ties to relatives and friends, travel, write, explore new skills, and volunteer to work for causes they believe in. Dan Sullivan does this in his own coaching, and he isn't a doctor. In his very first coaching session, he tells people how they can add years to their lives. (Dan, by the way, wants to live to age 156.) He gets them to put aside the mindset of inevitable decline and death and to go out and pursue their dreams.

More healthy years also allow people to pass on their wisdom, both about money and health, to their children and grandchildren. Most of my affluent clients built their wealth because they were hardworking and smart, not because they were lucky. It's a gift to the next generations if they can teach them good habits, attitudes, and strategies about money along with good habits, attitudes, and strategies about health.

We tend to work with the smart, successful, affluent client who has worked hard and gained a knowledge of money and investing but has not been happy with prior relationships in the money business. At my company, among the advisors, we have decades of experience as certified financial planners (CFPs). The typical advisor at my office is a CFP with a wealth of insurance and tax-planning knowledge. Also, we have a systematized, well-defined money management process, with plenty of access to our analysts and advisors. I conduct a live, monthly conference call with all my clients, and any one of them, of any net worth, can call in and get a live summary—not by email and not recorded earlier—of what has been going on in the market.

We provide a lot of services for our clients beyond financial planning and monitoring. We also

- work closely with tax preparers.
- find support professionals such as attorneys and CPAs as needed.
- coordinate with clients on instruments such as wills and trust funds.
- advise people on life insurance and long-term care insurance needs.
- help parents manage funding for their children's education.
- notify clients by mail if they cash out more than 5 percent of their holdings and when they need to start withdrawing funds from IRAs.

We reach out proactively, regularly asking clients if there's anything they need to talk about. We have a client event every year, a big party that allows clients to visit with advisors and vice versa, which helps build the sense of personal connection that so many people seek out. And we do all of this at competitive fees. In addition, we also offer a monthly conference call or Zoom or another video call regarding stock market and economic updates.

We know that people hate to be pressured into buying things, so if prospective clients reach out to us after they hear about Balanced Wealth, we give them a gentle sell. We call our first meeting with a client the discovery meeting, and there's no fee for that initial consult. They also don't have to worry about receiving multiple emails every day urging them to sign up for Balanced Wealth.

Once clients are enrolled in Balanced Wealth, they can determine how far they want to take the process. One client might want simply to fill in the scorecard every six months and share it with the CFP when they review the portfolio. Another may want to share the scorecard with their primary care physician and discuss it in detail during their annual checkup. A third client may want to fill in the scorecard twice a year but keep it to themselves, and that's their prerogative! The Balanced Wealth scorecard is an accountability partner review and checklist that integrates into the client's financial plan, and its prominence is up to the client. It can be a focus of discussion if that's what the client wants, or it can be handled with a quick conversation at the end of a semiannual review.

This is what happens when you call or email my firm, Capital Wealth Management:

You're greeted by our "director of first impressions." She'll ask you a few up front questions, such as your name, your occupation, what you have by way of investable assets, and how you heard of our firm. After the call, she will send you an email with a link to the calendar of one of our certified financial planners to schedule a "discovery meeting." Once the first meeting is scheduled, you'll receive an electronic form, where you can input your financial data and list your most important priorities. We'll also ask you to send helpful documents such as a tax return, brokerage statements, Social Security statements, and other records that demonstrate your income and assets. This information is for our eyes only and is completely secure within Capital Wealth Management; we don't share your data or sell it to any other entity.

At the discovery meeting, the CFP team member will cover the traditional categories of wealth management and ask you what areas you want to focus on. These include

- Retirement Income Analysis
- Portfolio review or a second opinion
- Estate Planning
- Tax Planning
- Insurance

- Charitable Planning
- Cash Flow Management/Budgeting

The CFP also will ask questions such as,

- What are your most pressing financial concerns?
- What type of lifestyle do you wish to enjoy during retirement?
- If you could change three things about your current financial situation, what would you change?
- What are your most important health and wellness objectives?

At this first meeting we might have you fill out a risk-tolerance questionnaire using a program called Riskalyze, but sometimes this is done at a subsequent meeting.

After the first meeting, the advisor analyzes the client tax return using Holistiplan software and enters your information into our financial-planning software, Right Capital. If Riskalyze was completed, the advisor will prepare a hypothetical investment allocation that falls within the parameters of your risk tolerance.

Once we determine those important aspects of your plan, we'll schedule a meeting to review the plan with you and present recommendations. Fees and charges, if applicable, will be discussed at that time. If you decide to work with us, we will prepare account paperwork and assist you in moving your assets to our firm. We'll have a follow-up meeting once your assets transfer over, so we can review accounts and confirm everything was moved correctly.

Once everything is in place, you are ready for the next step: the Balanced Wealth Scorecard, which is described in chapter 6. Once you've filled it out, you will also get a short list of basic medical questions, similar to what you might see on an insurance application. These are generic questions involving no specific personal data. The scorecard and the health questions get the conversation started, and a CFP reviews your concerns with you. At this point, we recommend that you visit your primary care provider. If you don't have one, this is a great time to check your insurance network and get an appointment with one. (Always consult your physician with the steps of Balanced Wealth and continue that process throughout your journey.) We'll discuss what's important to you in terms of wealth and health and establish a baseline for each.

If you're a Balanced Wealth client, we'll connect you to a nutritionist and a massage therapist, if necessary. Moreover, we will work with you to find the best place for you to pursue a workout routine, whether that's at a gym, dojo, yoga studio, Pilates center, or at home on your own equipment. We know more about workout alternatives in some cities than others, but we'll work with you to find the place that best suits your capabilities and needs. What matters most to us is that you can monitor your time spent and track your progress. If you seem to need help with sleep issues, we'll advise you to ask your primary care physician about visiting a sleep center. And we'll always be on top of the latest in precision medical care and wellness-tracking devices.

The scorecard, which should be updated every six months, is your accountability partner. Your planner at Capital Wealth Management will review it with you during our routine financial planning or asset management review, which occurs when you update the scorecard. You can track your progress, give feedback, and adjust as necessary in both the financial and wellness areas.

That's the Balanced Wealth process! Progress, not perfection, is your goal here, but you can count on us to keep pointing you in the right direction.

As I explained in chapter 2, there's a direct line between my sickly childhood and my current status, sixty years later, as a robust, energetic champion of wellness. The wheezing and coughing I suffered as an asthmatic kid surrounded by secondhand tobacco smoke gave me the impetus to become an adult who never had to take a sick day because I've always felt good. The steps I've taken as an adult—becoming involved in martial arts, leaving a job that would have required me to give up my physical regimen, taking up yoga, keeping on top of the latest trends in wellness and the latest technology to maintain it—plus a healthy dose of plain old good luck—are allowing me to experience my sixties as a much younger man might and to look forward to a long retirement filled with stamina and energy.

You might think, *That's nice for you, but you, sir, are an outlier. I don't have your money, connections, or ability to set my own hours.* But I'm not that unusual. *Anyone* can adopt a healthier lifestyle, track its components, and measure their progress. Mindful eating can cost no more than not eating junk food and walking costs nothing at all. Secondhand exercise equipment can be had for a song. The only connection you really need for exploring the world of wellness is Wi-Fi. For the price of a notebook or journal, you can track your food intake, your times and hours of sleep, the minutes you spent exercising, and your daily number of steps. And in the back of the notebook in which you keep your health records, you can write down your triggers for stress, your goals, your vision for the future.

The largest expenditure you'll make is *time*, but think of the time you spend as a substitution, not a sacrifice. Substitute record-keeping, menu-planning, and making food-shopping lists for the video games or puzzles you play on your phone while watching TV. Substitute a walk twice around the block for that first can of beer, an afternoon of hiking for an afternoon of shopping.

Whatever your age, situation, gender, or income level, I wish you a long and healthy life. I hope your quality of life allows you many more years of happiness with the people you love and the activities that fulfill you.

My success—and the success enjoyed by so many clients I've had the privilege of helping on their journey over the years—can be yours.

ACKNOWLEDGMENTS

Writing this book has been a lifelong dream come true, but it absolutely would not have been possible without the encouragement, direction, prayers, support, and the occasional kick in the butt from the wonderful team who came together to help me bring this book to life. I'd like to say a special word of thanks to:

Allen Harris, my developmental editor, who tirelessly helped a veteran writer break through writer's block and kept me on a weekly track that helped get this lifetime goal completed. Allen, you're amazing and gifted at helping people not only find their voice but helping them impact others by getting their message out.

Jonathan Merkh, Jen Gingerich, Lauren Ward, and Billie Brownell—my publishing team at Forefront Books. Thank you for your encouragement, project management, and publishing expertise in taking this author from the manuscript to a real, honest-to-goodness book people can read and use to change their lives! Justin Batt, your high energy, knowledge, and flexibility were the exact recipe I was looking for with this collaboration.

To my friends from Framingham, Massachusetts, since the fourth grade—you have all been gracious in your time and efforts. The dynamic duo of the Herrick brothers, Doug and Mark: your insightful comments and keen eyes for detail were greatly appreciated. Tony, your thoughts and feedback were extremely helpful and likely great material for a second book on this ever-growing and complex topic.

Carolyn Hine, your edits and deep dive on the first few chapters were awesome and right on target. Linda Champney, your encouragement early on and valuable feedback from a woman's perspective were so important. Peter Johanson, I am always energized and enlightened by our conversations on sleep, health, and wellness; your enthusiasm was always the push I needed to get to the next milestone in this process.

Mom, your steadfast attention to detail regarding the introduction and Dad's health history were crucial to setting the stage and building the narrative for my Balanced Wealth approach.

Peter Evans, your thoughts and feedback on the earlier drafts were so encouraging at a time when the project was in its infancy and just beginning to unfold.

Michael Levin, your wit, brevity, and keen grasp of the subject matter were immensely helpful throughout the entire process. I feel fortunate to have established a great friendship and an even better mentor in you.

For my team at Capital Wealth Management, LLC—my greatest thanks for your time, efforts, and unrelenting reading and rereading of the manuscript to get every detail correct. Jordan, Kelsey, Michael, and Kelly, without a doubt this manuscript exceeded my expectations because of your efforts.

Dan Sullivan, countless thanks for all you do for the entire worldwide community of entrepreneurs and for your guidance and feedback on my process. The FAST filter and our conversations about this project were very helpful. Most of all, the famous first Abundance trip in Boston in August 2021 was a complete game-changer and the catalyst for this book.

Lee Brower, your early suggestions and encouragement over a decade ago got me started on my first book, which has led me to this journey today. Moreover, your insights about combining my martial arts and health-related passions into the wealth management industry were prescient.

Peter Diamandis, much gratitude for all that you have taught and continue to teach us through the Abundance Longevity program. From BOLD Capital Partners through XPrize and everything in between, you continue to be a source of inspiration and innovation.

I would like to thank the following doctors who both reviewed the manuscript and/or gave me great feedback along the way:

Dr. Thomas Crabtree
Dr. Phil Defina
Dr. Michael Deshaies
Dr. Peter Diamandis
Dr. David Karow
Dr. Hector Lopez
L. Anne Maxwell, Ph.D.
Dr. Thomas Paloschi
Dr. George Shapiro
Dr. Marian Zanyk

NOTES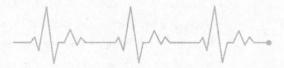

1. G. Kuhan and S. Raptis, " 'Trash foot' following operations involving the abdominal aorta," *Aust N Z J Surg,*
   67, no. 1 (January 1997): 21-24, https://pubmed.ncbi.
   nlm.nih.gov/9033371/.
2. *Mortality in the United States, 2020,* NCHS Data
   Brief No. 427, December 2021, https://www.cdc.gov
   /nchs/products/databriefs/db427.htm.
3. "Joyce Sunada," Marketplace eSpeakers, https://www
   .espeakers.com/marketplace/profile/26594/joyce
   -sunada.
4. Ginchin Funakoshi and Genwa Nakasone, *The Twenty
   Guiding Principles of Karate: The Spiritual Legacy of
   the Master* (Tokyo: Kodansha International, 2003).
5. Sophie Lewis, "Simone Biles says she feels the 'weight
   of the world' on her shoulders after tough Olympic qualifiers," CBS News, July 26, 2021, https://
   www.cbsnews.com/news/simone-biles-olympics
   -gymnastics-qualifiers/.

6. Deborah Borfitz, "Human Longevity Inc. Changing Healthcare 'One Patient at a Time,'" Diagnostic World, March 6, 2020, https://www.diagnosticsworld news.com/news/2020/03/06/human-longevity-inc .-changing-healthcare-one-patient-at-a-time.
7. "Treatment of Bladder Cancer, by Stage," American Cancer Society, https://www.cancer.org/cancer/bladder -cancer/treating/by-stage.html.
8. Borfitz, "Human Longevity Inc."
9. "Don't Die of Something Stupid," Peter H. Diamandis, podcast episode 53, May 13, 2018, https://www .diamandis.com/blog/podcast-episode-53-dont-die -from-something-stupid.
10. David Sinclair, *Lifespan: Why We Age—And Why We Don't Have To* (New York: Atria Books, 2019), 67.
11. Sinclair, *Lifespan*, 67.
12. "Disability Adjusted Life Years," Peterson-KFF Health System Tracker, https://www.healthsystemtracker .org/indicator/health-wellbeing/disability-adjusted -life-years/.
13. Brad McMillan, chief investment officer of Commonwealth Financial Networks in Waltham, MA, suggested drawing analogies between issues of financial planning and health management.
14. From a speech titled, "The Challenge of Central Banking in a Democratic Society" given to the American Enterprise Institute during the dot-com bubble of the 1990s.
15. "WinStreak," Strategic Coach, https://www.strategic-coach.com/get-the-app/.

16. Dan Sullivan, *The Gap and The Gain: Building Your Progress and Happiness Entirely on How Your Brain Works for You* (Strategic Coach, 2017), 15.

17. Matthew Walker, *Why We Sleep: Unlocking the Power of Sleep and Dreams* (New York: Scribner, 2017), 107.

18. "Lifestyle Interventions for Brain Health: Dr. Tanzi's 'SHIELD' Plan," Massachusetts General Hospital, McCance Center, https://www.massgeneral.org/neurology/mccance-center/clinic/shield.

19. John F. Kennedy, *Annual Message to the Congress on the State of the Union*, January 11, 1962, John F. Kennedy Presidential Library and Museum, https://www.jfklibrary.org/asset-viewer/archives/JFKPOF/037/JFKPOF-037-003.

20. David Shaywitz, "Peacetime vs Wartime CEO: A Useful Lens for Transformative Leaders?" *Timmerman Report*, March 7, 2022, https://timmermanreport.com/2022/03/peacetime-vs-wartime-ceo-a-useful-lens-for-transformative-leaders/.

21. "Hot or Cold: What's the Best Temperature for Sleep?" American Sleep Association Blog, www.sleepassociation.org/blog-post/best-temperature-for-sleep/.

22. "Why Doctor's Recommend the Mediterranean Diet," *HealthMatters*, New York-Presbyterian Hospital, https://healthmatters.nyp.org/why-doctors-recommend-the-mediterranean-diet-and-how-to-make-it-a-way-of-life/.

23. A good place to start is HelpGuide, a nonprofit health website: https://www.helpguide.org/articles/healthy-eating/healthy-eating.htm.

24. A comprehensive article from the National Institutes of Health can be found here: https://www.ncbi.nlm.nih.gov/pmc/articles/PMC6536904/. Harvard Health Publishing reports on recent changes in exercise guidelines: https://www.health.harvard.edu/blog/the-new-exercise-guidelines-any-changes-for-you-2018121415623. The American College of Sports Medicine offers numerous booklets on exercise at any age: https://www.acsm.org/education-resources/trending-topics-resources/physical-activity-guidelines.

25. HelpGuide lists these and many other hints for managing stress at https://www.helpguide.org/articles/stress/stress-management.htm.

26. "Microbiota-Gut-Brain Axis," Abstract, *Physiological Review*, August 28, 2019, https://journals.physiology.org/doi/full/10.1152/physrev.00018.2018?rfr_dat=cr_pub.

27. "Full Antonio Brown Meltdown," YouTube, January 2, 2022, https://www.youtube.com/watch?v=vlEfYfedKWg.

28. "Statement from Antonio Brown via his attorney @seanburstyn," Twitter, January 5, 2022, https://twitter.com/AdamSchefter/status/1478908618212884483?s=20&t=1SI2ajuRfp9POvUe6O8auQ.

29. Shiv Sudhaker, "Is Antonio Brown's meltdown a mental health cry for help?" Fox News, January 6, 2022, https://www.foxnews.com/sports/antonio-brown-meltdown-mental-health-cry-help.

30. Sudhaker, "Is Antonio Brown's meltdown a mental health cry for help?"

31. Elizabeth Forbes, "Football Legend Terry Bradshaw's Fight Against ADD & Depression," Hope to Cope, February 1, 2022, https://www.hopetocope.com /quaterback-scramble/.

32. Forbes, "Football Legend Terry Bradshaw's Fight."

33. Cathy Cassata, "Michael Phelps: 'My Depression and Anxiety Is Never Going to Just Disappear," Health- line, May 17, 2022, https://www.healthline.com /health-news/michael-phelps-my-depression-and -anxiety-is-never-going-to-just-disappear.

34. Rich Nye, "Colts owners 'Kicking the Stigma' of men- tal health illness," WTHR, May 3, 2021, https://www .wthr.com/article/news/health/colts-owners-kicking -the-stigma-of-mental-health-illness/531-77fd2c8e -106d-4cf4-8f58-fb7900661b51.

35. Gillian Zoe Segal, "Warren Buffet wants young peo- ple to know: Ignoring this is like 'leaving a car out in hailstorms,'" CNBC Make It, June 22, 2021, https:// www.cnbc.com/2019/04/12/billionaire-warren -buffett-greatest-advice-to-millennials-the-1-thing-in -life-you-need-to-prioritize.html.

36. Samuel G. Freedman, "Ruth Gordon, the Actress, Dies at 88," *The New York Times*, August 29, 1985, https://www.nytimes.com/1985/08/29/arts/ruth -gordon-the-actress-dies-at-88.html.

37. Tony Robbins, *Life Force: How New Breakthroughs in Precision Medicine Can Transform the Quality of Your Life & Those You Love* (New York: Simon & Schuster, 2022).

38. Dan Sullivan, "Why Finding Your Purpose Is the Key to Reaching Your Life Goals," Strategic Coach, https://resources.strategiccoach.com/the-multiplier -mindset-blog/why-finding-your-purpose-is-the-key -to-reaching-your-life-goals-3.

39. JD Hacker, "Decennial Life Tables for the White Population of the United States, 1790–1900," *Hist Methods*, April 2010, 43(2):45-79. doi: 10.1080/01615441003720449. PMID: 20563225; PMCID: PMC2885717, https://www.ncbi.nlm.nih .gov/pmc/articles/PMC2885717/.

40. Stephen Covey, "Work-Life Balance: A Different Cut," *Forbes*, March 21, 2007, https://www.forbes.com /2007/03/19/covey-work-life-lead-careers-worklife07 -cz_sc_0319covey.html?sh=7a2b2044754d.

41. Sullivan and Hardy, *The Gap and The Gain*, 54–55.

42. Jon Kabat-Zinn, *Arriving at Your Own Door: 108 Lessons in Mindfulness* (Paris: Hachette Books, 2007).